Life and Health Insurance

State Law Supplement

Important: Check for Updates

States sometimes revise their exam content outlines unexpectedly or on short notice. To see whether there is an update for this product because of an exam change, go to **www.kfeducation.com** and check the Insurance Licensing Blog. If there is an update, it will be clearly noted in the blog entries for this state.

Minnesota

Effective July 1, 2013

At press time, this edition contains the most complete and accurate information currently available. Owing to the nature of license examinations, however, information may have been added recently to the actual test that does not appear in this edition. Please contact the publisher to verify that you have the most current edition.

This publication is designed to provide accurate and authoritative information in regard to the subject matter covered. It is sold with the understanding that the publisher is not engaged in rendering legal, accounting, or other professional services. If legal advice or other expert assistance is required, the services of a competent professional should be sought.

MINNESOTA LIFE AND HEALTH INSURANCE LAW SUPPLEMENT, EFFECTIVE JULY 1, 2013
©2013 Kaplan, Inc.

If you find imperfections or incorrect information in this product, please visit www.kfeducation.com and submit an errata report.

Published in October 2013 by Kaplan Financial Education.

Printed in the United States of America.

ISBN: 978-1-4754-2192-7 / 1-4754-2192-3

PPN: 3200-4449

INTRODUCTION

This supplement focuses on statutes regarding Minnesota insurance law. Key aspects of each statute are discussed to help the student pass the state law portion of the licensing examination. In order to understand the content of this supplement, the student should first study the *Life, Accident, and Health License Exam Manual*. Thorough preparation for the exam requires the complete study of both the license exam manual and the supplement.

I. MINNESOTA LAWS, RULES, AND REGULATIONS COMMON TO LIFE, HEALTH, PROPERTY, AND CASUALTY INSURANCE

A. POWERS AND DUTIES OF THE COMMISSIONER [45; 60A.01-.031; 60K; 72A.02-.44; 62A.02; 61A.02; 79.2795; 72C.01-.02] The Department of Commerce is the regulatory authority for the Minnesota insurance industry. The governor appoints the Commissioner of Commerce, who has the power to examine and investigate the affairs of every person doing insurance business in Minnesota to determine whether the person has engaged in any unfair method of competition, or any unfair or deceptive practice.

1. Broad Powers The Commissioner is assigned broad powers and responsibilities regarding the regulation of insurance.

    a. The Commissioner is empowered to:
- enforce insurance laws;
- create rules that assist with the enforcement of insurance laws;
- conduct investigations and hold hearings to determine if any person has violated any insurance law or rule;
- examine and approve policy forms;
- examine the books, records, and documents of any person or entity engaged in regulated activity;
- publish information collected from investigations, hearings, and examinations;
- require reports of all sales or transactions that are regulated; and
- appoint a staff to assist with enforcement duties.

2. Examination of Records The Commissioner may examine the affairs and conditions of any licensed producer, license applicant, or foreign or domestic insurance company. This may be done at any time for any reason related to the enforcement of insurance laws, or to ensure that companies are operating in a safe and sound manner, and to protect the public interest. The Commissioner shall examine the affairs and conditions of every insurer licensed in Minnesota at least once every five years.

    a. Who may be examined The Commissioner, or person designated by the Commissioner, may examine any:
- company authorized to do business in Minnesota;
- person who is involved in the formation of an insurance company;

- licensed producer or solicitor or any person seeking a license; or
- person engaged in the business of adjusting losses or financing premiums.

b. **Purpose, scope, and notice of examination** In order to examine the records, the Commissioner must provide *notice of the scope* of the examination. A copy of the notice is sent to the examinee.

c. **Access to examinee** Once notice of the scope has been given, the insurer (or producer) must give *free access* to all books, records, and documents in question. Failure to submit to an examination is grounds for suspension, refusal, or nonrenewal of a producer's license or an insurer's authority to transact business in Minnesota.

   1.) When conducting an examination, the Commissioner may retain attorneys, appraisers, independent actuaries, or independent certified public accountants as examiners; the cost is paid by the company being examined.

d. **Examination report** Once the records have been examined, the Commissioner will issue an *examination report*. This report must contain a statement of findings and a summary of important points, recommendations, and suggestions. Once issued, this report can be used as evidence in any legal proceeding.

e. **Order** After the examination report has been issued, the Commissioner may also issue an *order*, which must be adhered to within the time specified. One or both of the following orders will be issued.

   1.) **Restore any deficiency** This order is issued if an insurance company's capital, surplus, or reserves becomes impaired.

   2.) **Cease and desist** This order is issued to prevent an insurer from transacting business that may harm the company's policyholders or the public.

f. **Penalty** Any person who violates or aids and abets any violation of a written order may be fined up to $10,000 for each day the violation continues.

3. **Notice and Hearing** If the insurer (or producer) disagrees with the Commissioner's findings, the insurer (or producer) has the right to request a hearing within 30 days of the order. Once the hearing has been requested, the Commissioner has another 30 days to hold the hearing.

4. **Forms and Rate Review** All schedules of policy premium rates, policies, certificates of insurance, notices of proposed insurance, applications for insurance, and endorsements and riders used in Minnesota must be filed with the Commissioner. All accident and health insurance policies must be filed with the Commissioner at least 60 days prior to use.

B. DEFINITIONS Insurance companies can be defined various ways based on where they are incorporated, what types of policies they sell, and who owns the company.

1. **Domestic and Foreign [60A.02]** Insurers are defined based upon the state in which they are incorporated.

    a. **Domestic** Any company that is incorporated or organized in the state of Minnesota.

    b. **Foreign** Any company that is incorporated or organized in another state that does business in Minnesota.

2. **Reciprocal [71A.01; 72A.41-.42]** Members of an unincorporated group insure each other and share the losses with each other. A reciprocal is managed by an attorney-in-fact who is empowered to handle all of the business of the reciprocal. Life insurance and ocean marine insurance are not acceptable risks for reciprocal exchanges.

3. **Stock and Mutual [60A; 67A]** Private insurance is sold by private sector insurance companies. This category of insurance includes most of the major types of insurance sold today, and includes life, health, property, and casualty policies. Stock and mutual insurers are the two main types of private insurers.

    a. **Stock insurers** Stock insurance companies sell insurance to the general public. Many stock insurers are large multi-national companies.

        1.) Stock companies are for-profit corporations that are owned by their shareholders.

        2.) Stock companies are managed by a board of directors.

        3.) Stock companies typically sell non-PAR (non-participating) policies. Policyholders are not eligible to receive insurance dividends. However, if the company is profitable, *shareholders* may receive taxable stock dividends. Occasionally, stock insurers will issue PAR policies to compete with mutual companies.

        4.) Stock companies issue non-assessable policies. They are required to set money aside in reserve in the event their claims experience is higher than anticipated. Non-assessable insurers are referred to as *legal reserve* companies.

    b. **Mutual insurers** Mutual insurance companies sell insurance to the general public. Like stock insurers, many mutual companies are also large multi-national organizations.

        1.) Mutual companies are not-for-profit corporations that are owned by their policyholders.

2.) Mutual companies are managed by a board of directors.

3.) Mutual companies sell PAR (participating) policies. PAR policies pay insurance dividends to policyholders if the insurer's revenue exceeds operating expenses and reserve requirements. These dividends are considered a refund of overpaid premium and are not taxable.

4.) Mutual companies are non-assessable insurers. As a result, they are considered to be legal reserve companies.

4. **Fraternals [64B.01, .05, .19]** A fraternal benefit society is not for profit and exists solely for the benefit of its members. It confines its membership to any one religious denomination, has a representative form of government, and is operated on a lodge system. Similar to other insurance companies operating in Minnesota, a fraternal benefit society must obtain a certificate of authority from the Commissioner and must abide by reserve and trade practice regulations. In addition, every society transacting business in Minnesota shall file an annual statement with the Commissioner reflecting its financial condition, transactions, and affairs for the previous year. Each contract owner will receive a certificate specifying the benefits provided. If the reserves drop below a certain level, or become impaired, the society may assess its members.

5. **Certificate of Authority [60A.07; 72A.41]** Insurance companies must obtain a certificate of authority to transact insurance business in the state of Minnesota. If an insurance company fails to do this, their insurance policies remain valid—to protect the public—but the company will face severe penalties.

   a. The following constitutes transacting insurance business:
   - Issuing or delivering a policy or annuity
   - Soliciting an application for insurance
   - Collecting premiums, fees, or assessments for a policy
   - Any other transaction related to an insurance policy

   b. An *admitted* carrier is an insurance company that has obtained a certificate of authority.

   c. Surplus lines companies may sell insurance in Minnesota without a certificate of authority, but they may only transact business through a licensed surplus lines agent. Companies without a certificate of authority are considered *non-admitted* carriers.

C. **LICENSING AND APPOINTMENTS [60K; 45.027; 60A.198; 2795.1200]** An individual may not sell, solicit, or negotiate insurance in Minnesota for any class of insurance unless the person is licensed for that line of authority. The license should be on display in the producer's office, and any reference to the license used in advertising may not infer endorsement nor sponsorship by state government.

1. **Education Requirements** Prior to obtaining an insurance producer license, an individual must complete a program of studies approved by the Commissioner and pass an examination.

    a. **Prelicensing** Individuals can complete their program of studies through classroom study or via the internet.

    1.) The course of study must consist of 20 hours per major line of authority in which the producer seeks to be licensed (Life, Accident and Health, Property, Casualty, Personal Lines).

    2.) The following are exempt from the prelicense education requirement:
    - Applicants with a two-year Minnesota vocational school degree in insurance
    - Applicants with a four-year college degree in business with an insurance emphasis
    - Life applicants with any of the following professional designations: CEBS, ChFC®, CIC, CFP®, CLU®, FLMI, or LUTCF
    - Health applicants with any of the following professional designations: RHU, CEBS, REBC, or HIA
    - Property, Casualty, or Personal Lines applicants with any of the following professional designations: AAI, ARM, CIC, or CPCU®

    3.) The course cannot be sponsored by, offered by, or affiliated with an insurance company.

    4.) Applicants who have been previously licensed for a particular line of insurance in the state of Minnesota do not need to repeat their prelicensing education for that line.

    5.) A certification of compliance from the education provider must accompany the applicant's license application.

    6.) Applicants must pass a written exam with a minimum passing score of 70%. The exam will test the knowledge of the individual concerning the lines of authority for which the application is made, the duties and responsibilities of an insurance producer, and the insurance laws and rules of Minnesota.

    7.) An applicant for a resident insurance producer license or a new line of authority must submit fingerprints for a criminal history background check and pay an associated fee.

    8.) Exam results are valid for three years from the date of the exam.

    9.) After completing prelicensing education and passing the applicable exam, applicants complete the license application online through a company called Sircon. Two fees apply: a license fee of $50 per line of authority, and a $25 technology fee.

10.) Minnesota law (M.S. 60K.365) now requires both resident and nonresident accident/health insurance producers selling long-term care policies in Minnesota to complete a one-time, eight-hour partnership course and a four-hour refresher course every two years after the initial training. Both courses can be completed as continuing education and, therefore, may be taken in either a classroom or through interactive distance learning through continuing education training sponsors.

b. Continuing Education Continuing education is required of producers licensed to sell lines of insurance for which an exam is required.

1.) Producers must complete a minimum of 24 credit hours of commissioner-approved courses during each two-year licensing period. At least three of those hours must be in a class or classes in the area of ethics.

2.) Only half the credit hours may be obtained through company-sponsored courses.

3.) Producers may take all continuing education hours via the internet or via other verifiable self-study.

4.) The education provider will provide the producer with a certification of compliance and also report the producer's continuing education hours to Sircon.

c. License Expiration

1.) Initial licenses issued to an individual producer on or after August 1, 2010 are valid for at least 12 months, but not more than 24 months; the license expires on the last day of the birth month within that 12- to 24-month period. Subsequent license periods are two years, and the license expires on the last day of the producer's birth month.

2. Types of Licenses Unless denied, individuals who have met the licensing requirements will be issued a two-year insurance producer license.

a. Producer A **resident producer's** license shall be issued to a person who resides in Minnesota or maintains their principal place of business in Minnesota. Individuals must:
- be at least 18 years of age;
- complete the necessary prelicensing education;
- pay the applicable fees;
- successfully pass the examination;
- not have committed any act that is grounds for license denial; and
- consent to a criminal history background check and fingerprinting.

1.) An individual insurance producer may receive a license in one or more of the following major lines:

- **Life insurance**—policies that insure human lives.
- **Accident and health insurance**—policies that provide coverage for sickness, income loss due to disability, and long-term care.
- **Property insurance**—policies that provide coverage for direct loss or damage to real property and personal property.
- **Casualty insurance**—policies that cover the insured's legal liability for injury to others and property damage of others.
- **Personal lines**—policies sold to individuals and families for primarily noncommercial purposes.
- **Variable life and variable annuity products insurance**—policies that provide coverage under variable life insurance contracts and variable annuities.

2.) An individual insurance producer may receive a license in one or more of the following limited lines:

- Limited line credit insurance
- Farm property and liability insurance
- Title insurance
- Travel insurance (new rules effective since 2012)
- Bail bonds

3.) The license must contain the licensee's name, address, producer license number, date of issuance, lines of authority, expiration date, and any other information the Commissioner considers necessary.

4.) The producer license remains in effect, unless revoked or suspended, as long as the fees are paid, continuing education requirements are met, and all necessary documentation is provided to the Commissioner by the renewal date.

5.) A licensed producer who is unable to comply with license renewal procedures due to military service, or some other extenuating circumstance, such as a long-term medical disability, may request a waiver of those procedures. The producer may also request a waiver of any examination requirement or any other fine or sanction imposed for failure to comply with renewal procedures.

6.) The Commissioner may issue a temporary producer license, not to exceed 180 days, without requiring an exam in the following circumstances:

- To the surviving spouse or court-appointed personal representative of a deceased or disabled licensed producer to allow adequate time for the sale of the business, or the producer's recovery, or the licensing of a replacement

- To an employee of a business entity licensed as a producer, upon the death or disability of the individual designated on the license
- To the designee of a licensed producer entering active service in the armed forces of the United States
- In any other circumstance that serves the public interest

b. Nonresident [60K.39] A nonresident of Minnesota shall receive a **nonresident producer license** if the person is currently licensed as a resident and is in good standing in their home state; has submitted the proper request for a license and paid the required fees; has submitted to the Commissioner the license application submitted to their home state, or in lieu of that, a completed Uniform Application; and the person's home state awards nonresident producer licenses to Minnesota residents on the same basis.

1.) The Commissioner may verify the producer's licensing status through the NAIC producer database.

2.) A nonresident producer who moves from one state to another must file a change of address and provide certification from the new resident state within 10 days of legal residence. No fee or license application is required.

3.) A nonresident producer license terminates automatically when the person's resident license is terminated for any reason.

4.) Persons licensed as a surplus lines producer in their home state will receive a nonresident surplus lines producer license in Minnesota, and persons licensed as a limited lines producer in their home state will receive a nonresident limited lines license in Minnesota.

c. Agency A business entity acting as an insurance producer is required to obtain an insurance producer license using the Uniform Business Entity Application.

1.) The business must:
- pay the applicable fees; and
- designate an individual licensed producer responsible for the business entity's compliance with Minnesota insurance laws and rules.

2.) Each person who is affiliated with the agency and who is personally engaged in the sale or solicitation of insurance must also be licensed individually.

d. Managing General Agent A managing general agent (MGA) hires producers, supervises a territory, is responsible for agent activities, and must be licensed as an insurance producer.

e. Surplus Lines [60A.198] A surplus lines license allows the producer to place insurance risks with eligible surplus lines insurers.

1.) A Minnesota licensed producer may obtain a surplus lines license by completing an application, registering with the Surplus Lines Association of Minnesota, and paying a fee.

2.) Prior to placing insurance with an eligible surplus lines insurer, a surplus lines licensee must inform the insured that coverage is being placed with an insurer not licensed in Minnesota, and that payment of a loss is not guaranteed in the event of insolvency of the surplus lines insurer.

f. Exceptions to licensing The following entities are not required to be licensed as an insurance producer:

1.) Any officer, employee, or secretary of a fraternal benefit society who devotes substantially all their time to other activities and who receives no commission.

2.) An officer, director, or employee of an insurer or producer who does not receive commission on policies sold in Minnesota and:

a.) whose duties are executive, managerial, or clerical in nature and are indirectly related to the sale, solicitation, or negotiation of insurance;

b.) whose job function relates to underwriting, loss control, or adjusting claims; or

c.) who serves in the capacity of a special producer where the person's activities are limited to providing technical assistance to licensed producers.

3.) A person who collects information, takes enrollments, issues certificates, or performs administrative services for group life, property and casualty, annuities, or accident and health insurance and receives no commission for the services.

4.) An employer or association or its officers, directors, employees, or the trustees of an employee trust plan who administer its employee benefit program and who are not compensated by the insurer issuing the contracts.

5.) Employees of insurers who inspect, rate, or classify risks or train producers and who do not sell, solicit, or negotiate insurance.

6.) A person whose activities are limited to advertising and not selling, soliciting, or negotiating insurance.

7.) A salaried, full-time employee who advises an employer on insurance matters if the employee does not sell or solicit insurance or receive commission.

8.) Formerly, employees of rental car companies offering insurance when renting a car did not need to be licensed. New definitions of travel insurance (SF2069) now ask entities to be licensed and follow certain procedures.

3. Termination of License

a. **Expiration** An individual producer may voluntarily surrender a license by choosing not to renew it.

b. **Revocation or Suspension [60K.43]** The Commissioner may restrict, censure, suspend, revoke, or refuse to issue or renew an insurance producer's license, or levy a civil penalty or any combination of actions.

   1.) The Commissioner may take action against an individual for any one or more of the following:
   - Providing incorrect, misleading, incomplete, or materially untrue information on an application for an insurance license
   - Violating the insurance laws or regulations of the State of Minnesota or any other state
   - Attempting to obtain an insurance license through fraud or misrepresentation
   - Improperly withholding, misappropriating, or converting money or property received in the course of doing insurance business
   - Misrepresenting the terms of an actual or proposed insurance policy
   - Being convicted of, or pleading guilty to or no contest to, a felony, gross misdemeanor, or misdemeanor involving moral turpitude
   - Committing any unfair trade practice or fraud
   - Using fraudulent, coercive, or dishonest practices
   - Demonstrating incompetence, untrustworthiness, or financial irresponsibility
   - Having an insurance license in any jurisdiction denied, suspended, revoked, or subject to fine, and being disciplined for any reason
   - Committing forgery, whether or not the forgery is related to an insurance transaction
   - Cheating on an insurance license exam
   - Knowingly accepting insurance business from an individual who is not licensed
   - Failing to make court-ordered child support payments
   - Failing to pay state income taxes
   - Being enjoined by any court of competent jurisdiction from engaging in any aspect of the insurance business

■ Making any communication to a potential buyer that the producer is acting on behalf of a government agency

■ Violating any notification, disclosure, or record-keeping requirement, or any standard of conduct imposed by Minnesota statute while performing residential mortgage activity

2.) The Commissioner may issue an order for a hearing, requiring the licensee to show why the license should not be censured, suspended or revoked, or why a civil penalty should not be imposed.

3.) If the Commissioner non-renews or denies a license application, the Commissioner must notify the person in writing of the reason.

   a.) The applicant or licensee has 30 days to file a written request for a hearing to determine the reasonableness of the Commissioner's action.

   b.) The hearing must be held within 30 days, and will be in front of an administrative law judge.

   c.) The applicant or licensee may appeal the judge's decision directly to the Minnesota Court of Appeals.

4.) The license of a business entity may be suspended, revoked, or refused if the Commissioner finds, after a hearing, that an individual licensee's violation was known, or should have been known, by one or more of the partners or managers, and the violation was not reported to the Commissioner in a timely manner.

5.) A license is *suspended* for any period of not less than three months. The producer may not sell or service insurance policies during the suspension.

6.) A person whose license is *revoked* is prohibited from license reapplication for at least two years from the effective date of the revocation. As a condition of reapplication the producer must obtain a performance bond of at least $20,000 with the state of Minnesota as obligee. The bond must be filed with the Commissioner.

7.) If the Commissioner suspends, revokes, or terminates a license, the Commissioner must notify the producer and all appointing insurers. Upon notification the producer must immediately deliver their license to the Commissioner.

8.) A person whose license has been revoked, suspended, or denied may not transact any insurance business during that time.

9.) In addition to taking action against a producer's license, the Commissioner may fine a producer up to $10,000 per violation.

4. **Appointment [60K.49-.51]** A licensed producer is at all times the agent of the insurer not the insured, and has a fiduciary responsibility to the insurer. The producer must always protect the insurer's interests and follow any lawful instructions from the insurer. When insurance companies *appoint* producers to act on their behalf they are responsible for all acts of the producer when that producer is acting within the scope of the producer's authority.

   a. A licensed insurance producer shall not transact insurance business on behalf of an insurer unless the producer either has:
      ■ been appointed by the insurer; or
      ■ the insurer's permission to transact business on its behalf and obtains an appointment within 15 days after submitting the first application to the insurer.

   b. To appoint a producer as its agent, the insurer must file a notice of appointment within 15 days from the date the agency contract is executed or submission of the first insurance application. Insurers may only appoint licensed producers, and must pay an appointment fee for each producer appointed.

   c. Upon receipt of the notice, the Commissioner will verify within 30 days that the producer is eligible for appointment. If the producer is ineligible for appointment, the Commissioner shall notify the insurer within five days.

   d. A company appointment will remain in force until voluntarily terminated by the insurer or producer, or until the producer's license has been terminated for any reason.

   e. An insurer may not knowingly appoint a producer whom the insurer knows has committed misconduct or is otherwise unqualified or unfit. Upon discovery of this, the insurer must immediately terminate the appointment and notify the Commissioner. No insurer shall employ a producer whose license has been revoked.

   f. The *agency agreement* is the legal agreement that establishes the relationship between the insurer and producer, and outlines the powers and responsibilities of the producer. While acting on behalf of the insurer, the producer has three levels of authority:

      1.) Express authority is extended to the producer as part of the agency agreement and allows the producer to complete all necessary job functions.

      2.) Implied authority is authority not extended to the producer as part of the agency agreement but is authority necessary to complete the functions allowed in the agency agreement.

      3.) Apparent authority is authority not extended by the agency agreement but is authority that a reasonable person would presume the producer has.

5. Termination of Appointment [60K.51]

a. An insurer that terminates a company appointment for any reason must notify the Commissioner within 30 days following the effective date of the termination.

b. Within 15 days of notifying the Commissioner, the insurer must send written notice of the termination to the producer.

c. Within 30 days after receiving notice of the termination, the producer may file written comments concerning the termination with the Commissioner. The comments become part of the Commissioner's file and must accompany every report distributed or disclosed about the producer.

d. Any insurer that fails to file a company appointment is penalized $25 per offense. Each sale of a policy by an unappointed producer is a separate offense. The maximum penalty per unappointed producer is $300.

e. If the insurer fails to pay a penalty within 10 days after notice from the Commissioner, the insurer's authority to transact business in Minnesota will be revoked until the penalty is paid.

6. Maintenance and Duration of License
Insurance producer licenses are valid for a period of 24 months. The license remains in effect unless revoked or suspended as long as the producer meets continuing education requirements and pays the applicable renewal fees.

a. Notification requirements A licensee is required to give written notice to the Commissioner in the following situations:

1.) Change of name or address The producer must notify the Commissioner within 10 days of a change of name, address, or any other information that was provided on the initial license application.

2.) Administrative actions The producer must notify the Commissioner of any administrative action taken against the producer in another jurisdiction, or by another Minnesota governmental agency within 30 days of the final disposition of the matter. The report must include a copy of the order and any other relevant legal documents.

3.) Criminal prosecutions The producer must notify the Commissioner of any criminal prosecution against the producer in any jurisdiction. This notification shall be made within 30 days of the initial pre-trial hearing date, and shall include a copy of the initial complaint and any other relevant legal documents.

4.) Criminal convictions and guilty pleas The producer must notify the Commissioner within 10 days of any conviction, guilty plea, or plea of no contest to any felony, gross misdemeanor, or misdemeanor involving moral turpitude.

5.) Assumed names A producer doing business under any name other than the legal name (e.g., Summit Insurance Services) must properly file the name with the Secretary of State. Once the assumed name has been filed, the producer must provide the Commissioner with documentation showing the proper filing before using the name.

b. Reinstating a lapsed license An individual producer whose license lapses may, within 12 months from the due date of the renewal fee, reinstate the license without having to pass a written exam. However, a penalty of twice the unpaid renewal fee must be paid to reinstate the license.

D. TRADE PRACTICES [60K; 72A.20; 2790; 2795.1200] Several statutes regulate and prohibit unfair trade practices in the insurance industry by defining all practices that constitute unfair methods of competition, or unfair or deceptive acts or practices. Penalties levied against insurers and producers include action against the license, fines, and criminal penalties.

1. Prohibited Practices Methods, acts, and practices that are defined as unfair or deceptive.

a. Rebating [72A.08]—offering or giving any rebate of premiums, dividends, stock, bonds or securities, or anything else of value as an inducement to buy insurance. A promotional advertising item or gift of $25 or less per year is not a rebate if the receipt of the item or gift is not conditioned on purchase of a policy or product. The penalty is $60 to $200 per violation.

b. Misrepresentation—making statements that misrepresent the policies, dividends, or financial condition of any insurer, particularly for the purpose of inducing a policyholder to lapse, forfeit, or surrender an insurance policy.

c. Defamation—making, publishing, or circulating any oral or written statement that is false, or is maliciously critical of, or derogatory to, the financial condition of an insurer, and that is intended to injure any person engaged in the business of insurance.

d. Discrimination—making or permitting any unfair discrimination between individuals in the same class of insureds when setting rates, or refusing to offer, sell, or renew coverage, or limiting coverage on the basis of marital status, gender, a disability, or because the proposed insured is a victim of domestic abuse.

e. Discrimination of military personnel—refusing to insure or continue to insure the life of a National Guard or armed forces reserve member due to that person's status as a member is an unfair and deceptive act unless the individual has received an order for active duty. In addition, if coverage for a National Guard or armed forces reserve member was terminated, cancelled, or nonrenewed while that person was on active duty, an insurer may not refuse to reinstate coverage for the insured or any covered dependents under an individual or group life or health policy. The person shall apply for reinstatement within 90 days after removal from active duty.

f. Misappropriation of funds—improperly withholding, misappropriating or converting funds belonging to a policyholder, beneficiary, or other person.

g. False advertising—making any oral or written statement with respect to the business of insurance, or with respect to any person in the conduct of the person's insurance business that is untrue, deceptive, or misleading.

h. Boycott, coercion, and intimidation—any act of boycott, coercion, or intimidation resulting in an unreasonable restraint of, or monopoly in, the business of insurance.

i. False financial statements—making or filing any false financial statement of an insurer with the intent to deceive.

j. Twisting—replacing insurance to the detriment of the insured.

k. Forgery—committing forgery, whether or not the forgery is related to an insurance transaction.

l. Suitability—when recommending the purchase of insurance, the producer must make reasonable inquiries to determine suitability.

m. Penalties [72A.03, .04] In addition to administrative penalties levied by the Commissioner, the following criminal penalties apply when violating insurance laws:

   1.) The first offense is a misdemeanor; each subsequent offense is a gross misdemeanor.

   2.) The following offenses are a gross misdemeanor on the first offense:
   - Acting as an insurance producer without a valid license
   - Making false statements on an insurance application
   - Forging the signature of another person

n. Unfair claims settlement methods and practices [72A.201]

   1.) The insurer may not delay or refuse to settle a claim because the claimant retains an attorney or public adjuster.

   2.) The insurer may not demand irrelevant information that has nothing to do with the loss.

   3.) The insurer must adopt reasonable standards for the prompt investigation of a claim.

   4.) The insurer may not refuse to pay a claim unless the insurer conducts a reasonable investigation.

5.) The insurer may not compel an insured to commence litigation by offering an inadequate settlement.

6.) The insurer may not make the settlement of one part of a claim contingent upon the insured's agreement to settle another part of the claim.

7.) The insurer may not deny a claim without disclosing the specific policy provision that applies to the claim denial.

8.) The insurer must have reasonable evidence and documentation to support any comparative negligence assignment.

9.) The insurer may not deny a claim because the insured did not *officially* report it or use the proper forms, nor settle based on an application that was altered without notice, knowledge, or consent of the insured.

10.) The insurer may not refuse to pay a claim because the insured might collect for damages under a different policy.

11.) The insurer may not require inspections at specific places or distances unreasonable for the insured to travel.

12.) The insurer must reply to customer claims and inquiries within 10 days.

13.) The insurer must identify the coverage under which all claim payments are made.

2. Compensation of Licensees [60K.48]

a. An insurer or producer may not pay a *commission* or other valuable consideration to a person for selling or negotiating insurance in Minnesota if that person is required to be licensed and is not licensed.

b. A person may not accept a commission or other valuable consideration for selling or negotiating insurance in Minnesota if that person is required to be licensed and is not licensed.

c. Renewal or other deferred commission may be paid to a retired producer for policies that were sold while the person was licensed.

d. A licensed producer may not charge *fees for service* unless all fees are reasonable and fully disclosed in writing. Before providing services, the producer must provide a written statement disclosing the amount of the fees, the services for which fees are charged, and if the fees are charged in addition to premiums.

3. Advertising and Marketing Standards [60A; 72A.20; 2790; 61B.28 subd. 4]
Minnesota statutes regulate insurance advertising and marketing to ensure that communication of insurance products is clear and complete.

a. Advertising is defined to include the following:
- Printed and published material
- Audiovisual material
- Descriptive literature
- Radio and television
- Billboards
- Circulars and leaflets
- Form letters
- Prepared sales talks and presentations

b. Advertising and marketing standards Advertisements or representations may not contain deceptive words, phrases, or illustrations. In addition, producers must abide by certain sales practices when transacting business to avoid misleading or deceiving the public.

1.) No written or oral advertisement may omit words, phrases, statements, references, or illustrations.

2.) An advertisement may not use words or phrases such as *all, full, complete, comprehensive, unlimited, up to,* or *as high as* to exaggerate any benefits beyond the terms of the policy.

3.) Also prohibited are the phrases *this policy will help pay your medical bills,* or *replace your income,* or *fill the gaps of your current insurance* when expressing loss of time benefits.

4.) Words such as *extra cash* or *extra income* may not be used to imply the receipt of benefits in excess of medical expenses.

5.) Advertisements may not use words such as *free, no cost, no additional cost* with respect to any benefit unless true or accurate.

6.) Dividends are a return of premium and may not be referred to as tax-free.

7.) A policy covering only one disease or a list of specified diseases must not imply coverage beyond the policy terms. A particular disease may not be referred to by more than one name to imply broader coverage.

8.) All policy limitations must be disclosed.

9.) Maximum benefits may not be emphasized with the intent to minimize any limits or other policy conditions.

10.) Benefit examples must be clear and must be shown only for losses from common illnesses or injuries rather than exceptional or rare conditions.

11.) An advertisement must not state that the insurer *pays for financial needs, safeguards your standard of living, guarantees your paycheck or income,* or uses similar words or phrases unless true.

12.) Advertisements may not state that premiums will not change unless it is true.

13.) If the policy states benefits and premiums, it must also state policy deductibles.

14.) The advertisement must clearly define how other insurance may apply and disclose any overlapping benefits.

15.) Publications must fully disclose the costs of premium financing (annual, semi-annual, quarterly, or monthly).

16.) Any waiting period due to preexisting conditions must be disclosed.

17.) It is unfair and deceptive to use the terms *investment, investment or expansion plan, profit,* or *profit-sharing* in connection with life insurance, annuities, or endowment contracts.

18.) The term *life insurance* must appear on the policy name or title to clearly indicate the policy is a life insurance, annuity, or endowment contract.

19.) Insurers may not infer that the insured is also a stockholder in the insurance company or will acquire stock ownership.

20.) No statement or reference may imply that by purchasing an insurance policy, the insured will become a member of a limited group of persons who may receive special advantages or additional dividends, unless such benefits are provided in the policy.

21.) Insurers may not state or imply that only a limited number of persons are eligible to buy a particular policy unless the limitation is verified by the insurer's underwriting practices.

22.) An advertisement must not state or imply that the insurer and its products are approved, endorsed, or accredited by the state or federal government.

23.) No one may publish in any way an advertisement, announcement, or statement, written or oral, which uses the existence of the Minnesota Life and Health Insurance Guaranty Association for the purpose of sales, solicitation, or inducement to purchase any form of insurance. It is not a violation of this subdivision to explain verbally to an applicant the coverage provided by the Minnesota Life and Health Insurance Guaranty Association at any time during the application process or thereafter.

24.) An advertisement must not make unfair or incomplete comparisons of policies, or unfairly disparage competitors or their products.

4. Agent and Insurance Company Conduct [2700; 2790; 2795; 72A; 72C]

a. Agent conduct

1.) When recommending the purchase of insurance, the producer must make reasonable inquiries to determine suitability. The customer's income, insurance needs, and any existing policies compared to recommended policies must be analyzed.

2.) Producers may accept a loan from an individual with whom the producer met in the course of the producer's business, provided the loan agreement is in writing. All records relating to the loan must be kept on file for at least six years after repayment.

3.) Policies must be delivered or mailed to the insured within 30 working days of the producer's receipt from the insurer.

4.) A written receipt must be issued anytime a producer takes possession of an insured's, or potential insured's, policies, certificates, or other insurance documents. The signed and dated receipt must contain an itemized list of the materials received, and the producer's name, address, and telephone number.

5.) A producer who is convicted of a felony, gross misdemeanor, or misdemeanor involving moral turpitude must report it to the Commissioner within 10 working days of the conviction.

6.) Any producer whose insurance, securities, or real estate license is suspended or revoked in another state, or has been ordered to pay a civil penalty because of misconduct in those industries, must report the disciplinary action to the Commissioner within 10 working days of the effective date of the action.

7.) Every producer must observe high standards of commercial honor in the conduct of their business.

8.) Every licensed resident producer must maintain a registered office for service of process. The address must be specified on all license and renewal applications.

9.) A license must be displayed in the licensee's office in a place where it can readily be viewed and inspected.

10.) A producer holding client funds must provide an itemized statement showing the amount of money held.

11.) Financial and complaint records must be kept on file for six years.

12.) A producer who receives a policy cancellation request must make or initiate the refund within 10 days of the request. Refunds must be delivered or mailed to the insured within five days of the producer's receipt from the insurer.

13.) If the producer is a financial planner, the producer must disclose all professional licenses held and the producer's compensation method (e.g., commission or fee).

b. Insurance company conduct

1.) Complaint records must be retained for four years after the complaint is made and must contain adequate information for easy retrieval.

2.) Policy forms, applications, and advertising must be retained for three years after the effective date.

3.) Claim records must be retained for three years after the claim is paid or denied.

4.) Automatic enrollment for any coverage in addition to that already in force is prohibited without the customer's consent.

5.) Discrimination due to a visual impairment is prohibited.

6.) Insurance policies must be readable and understandable to a person of average intelligence, experience, and education. A readable policy has:
- simple sentence structure and short sentences;
- commonly used and understood words;
- minimal legal terms; and
- minimal references to other sections or provisions of the policy.

7.) All policies must pass the *Flesch scale analysis*, which measures the ease of readability. Policies are analyzed for the number of syllables per word, and the number of words per sentence.

8.) All advertisements are the responsibility of the insurer. Insurers must establish and maintain a system of control over the content, form, and method of advertisements. This system would include prior approval requirements for any advertising by its agents and representatives.

9.) Upon policy termination, all unearned premium must be delivered to the insured within 30 days following the insurer's receipt of the insured's cancellation request.

5. Required Disclosures [60K.46; 60A.08] Anytime a licensed producer has contact with a prospective client, the producer is legally obligated to disclose certain information.

a. Personal solicitation of sales Prior to a personal solicitation, the producer, or a person acting on behalf of the producer, must disclose the following in writing:

- Their name
- The insurance company or agent they represent
- The fact that they are in the business of selling insurance

1.) If the initial personal contact is made by telephone, the producer can disclose the information verbally.

2.) A personal solicitation is defined as a sale, or attempted sale, by a producer or a person acting on behalf of a producer. This applies whether the contact is made in person, by telephone, or by electronic means.

3.) The best way to comply with the requirement is to have the necessary information printed on the producer's business cards.

  a.) If the producer does not use business cards, the required information can be added to applications or financial planner disclosure forms.

  b.) If the producer represents several companies, the producer can provide a business card that includes the producer's name and sufficient information for a reasonable person to determine that the producer is in the business of selling insurance.

4.) Any material that relates to specific insurance products must include the identity of the insurer. This material includes applications, brochures, policy illustrations, and binders.

5.) Producers must obtain the explicit permission of the insured before disclosing to any other person that the insured is a customer of the producer.

6.) Oral binders must be followed up in writing to the insured within five business days.

b. Fees for services All fees charged must be reasonable in relation to the services provided. Any producer who charges service fees must disclose the following in writing:

- The services for which the fees are charged

■ The amount of the fees

■ The fact that the fees are charged in addition to premiums

■ That premiums include a commission

c. Fair Credit Reporting Act

1.) With permission of the potential applicant, insurance companies use various sources of information in their underwriting process. In addition to the application, insurers use the applicant's:

■ driving records provided by the Department of Motor Vehicles;

■ medical records provided by the applicant's physician; and

■ credit reports provided by a consumer reporting agency that include the applicant's credit standing, occupation, finances, and marital status.

2.) The Fair Credit Reporting Act protects consumers by requiring that the insurer notify the consumer when the insurer accesses the consumer's credit report, and advise how the consumer can correct information on the report. It also ensures that credit reporting agencies exercise their responsibilities in a fair and impartial way.

3.) When a credit report is ordered, the applicant must be notified both verbally and in writing of the following.

a.) The applicant has the right to request a copy of the report from the credit agency.

b.) The applicant may request to be interviewed.

c.) The applicant has the right to challenge any erroneous information contained in the report. Any challenge must be made directly to the credit agency, who must respond to the challenge within 30 days.

d.) The applicant may make a written statement regarding any negative information in the credit report. The credit agency must include this statement in the credit report.

4.) Most adverse information remains in a credit report for seven years. Bankruptcy information remains in the report for 10 years.

d. Gramm-Leach-Bliley Act
The Gramm-Leach-Bliley Act requires insurance companies to disclose their privacy policy, and how a customer's personal (non-public) information may be used and shared with affiliates and third parties. The Act requires companies to provide their privacy policy when a policy is issued, and at least once a year thereafter.

E. **GUARANTY ASSOCIATION [61B;60C]** The purpose of the Minnesota Insurance Guaranty Association is to protect policyholders from an insurer's inability to pay claims due to insolvency or bankruptcy. The Association will pay unpaid claims up to certain maximums limited by Minnesota statute. The protection provided is based on Minnesota law, and the language of the insolvent company's policies at the time of insolvency. Funding of the Guaranty Association comes from contributions made by admitted carriers. The Minnesota Life and Health Insurance Guaranty Association shall establish and maintain two accounts: the life insurance and annuity account and the health insurance account.

   1. **Notice of Policyholder Rights** The notice of policyholder rights must be given either at the time of application; if the application is not taken in person, notice must be sent within 72 hours of taking the application, or may be given at delivery.

   2. It is an unfair trade practice for any insurer or producer to use the protection afforded by the Guaranty Association as a reason for buying insurance.

II. MINNESOTA LAWS, RULES, AND REGULATIONS PERTINENT TO LIFE INSURANCE ONLY [61A; 62B; 72A.51-.52]

   A. **BENEFICIARIES [61A.04; .12]** The beneficiary is the person(s) named by the policyowner to receive the death benefit; the beneficiary has several options from which to choose once eligible to receive the payment. The beneficiary can receive the death benefit in a single lump sum payment, in installments, or can leave the money on deposit with the insurance company.

   1. **Protection from Creditors** If the beneficiary is eligible to receive the death benefit, but chooses to leave part or all of the money on deposit with the insurance company, the money is protected from the claims of the beneficiary's creditors.

   2. **Policyowner Rights** The **spendthrift provision** is an additional provision used when the policy provides monthly, quarterly, semiannual, or annual payments to the beneficiary. It states that all rights of the beneficiary to commute, change the installment amount or time of payment, surrender for cash, borrow against, or assign the policy are withdrawn, and the parts of the policy giving the beneficiary those rights are voided. The intent of the policy is that the beneficiary shall have no rights under the contract except to receive the benefit in the installment amount, and at the time, stated in the policy.

   B. **RIGHT TO CANCEL [72A.51-.52]** The insured has the right to cancel a life insurance policy or annuity, but must do so within a specified period of time. The insurer must include a notice in the policy about cancellation and the return of premiums to the insured.

   1. **Insured** The policyowner may cancel the policy by returning it and giving written notice of cancellation within 10 days of receiving the policy. This is also called the *free-look* period.

    a. Notice of cancellation and return of the policy may be given personally or by mail. If by mail, the notice or policy return is effective upon being postmarked, properly addressed, and postage prepaid.

    b. Upon cancellation, the policyowner is entitled to a full refund within 10 days after the cancellation notice and returned policy are received by the insurer or its agent. A return of a variable insurance policy might not return the entire premium paid.

    c. Cancellation of an insurance policy makes the policy void from its inception.

2. **Insurance Company** In addition to all other legal requirements, the policy shall show the insurer's name and address, the seller of the policy, and shall include a notice regarding the insurer's actions and the policyowner's rights related to policy cancellation.

    a. The notice, which must be clear and conspicuous, shall contain the following elements regarding policy cancellation.

        1.) The policyowner has a minimum of 10 days to cancel the policy beginning on the date the policy is received by the owner.

        2.) If the policy is a replacement policy, the policyowner has a minimum of 30 days to cancel beginning on the date the policy is received by the owner. This requirement may also be provided in a separate written notice that is delivered with the policy.

        3.) A requirement for the return of the policy to the company or an agent of the company.

        4.) A statement that, if cancelled, the policy is considered void from the beginning.

        5.) A statement that the insurer will refund all premiums paid, including any fees or charges, if the policy is returned.

        6.) A statement describing when the cancellation becomes effective.

    b. The insurer must return all payments made for the policy within 10 days after it receives notice of cancellation and the returned policy.

    c. If a policy is sold without the notice regarding cancellation, it may be cancelled by the purchaser at any time within one year after the purchase date by returning it and giving written notice of cancellation to the insurer or its agent. If a purchaser cancels a policy under these conditions, the insurer must return the entire consideration paid within 10 days after receiving notice of cancellation and the returned policy.

C. POLICY PROVISIONS No life insurance policy may be issued in Minnesota or by a life insurance company organized under Minnesota law unless it contains several standard provisions. The grace period provision allows the policy to remain in force even if the premium payment is late.

1. **Grace Period [61A.03 subd 1(b)]** Provides a one-month grace period after the premium due date for the policyowner to make the payment, during which the insurance will continue in force. The provision may subject the late payment to a finance charge and contain a stipulation that if the insured dies during the grace period, the overdue premium will be deducted from any settlement.

D. BACK DATING [61A.07(3); 72A.52] Minnesota law allows for a life insurance policy to be issued, or to take effect up to six months before the original application date. This applies to policies issued or delivered in Minnesota, or issued by a life insurance company organized under Minnesota law.

1. **Selling to persons age 65 or older [61A.071]** No individual life insurance policy shall be issued or delivered in Minnesota to a person age 65 or older unless a signed and completed copy of the application for insurance is left with the applicant at the time application is made. This requirement does not apply to life insurers who mail a copy of the signed, completed application to the applicant within 24 hours of receiving the application. However, if an individual life policy is marketed on a direct response basis, a copy of any application signed by the applicant shall be delivered to the insured along with, or as part of, the policy.

E. CREDIT INSURANCE (LIFE AND A&H) [62B.02-.04] **Credit life insurance** is insurance on the life of a debtor (borrower) in connection with a specific loan. **Credit accident and health insurance** is insurance on a debtor to provide indemnity for payments due on a specific loan while the debtor is disabled.

1. **Forms of credit insurance** Credit life and credit accident and health insurance can be issued only in the following forms:

   a. Individual term life insurance policies issued to debtors

   b. Individual accident and health insurance policies issued to debtors, or disability benefit provisions in individual credit life insurance policies

   c. Group term life insurance policies issued to creditors providing insurance upon the lives of debtors

   d. Group accident and health insurance policies issued to creditors insuring debtors, or disability benefit provisions in group credit life insurance policies

2. **Amount of credit insurance**

   a. **Credit life insurance**

      1.) The initial amount of credit life insurance shall not exceed the amount of principal repayable, plus an amount equal to one monthly payment.

    2.) If the term of the loan exceeds 63 months, the amount of credit life insurance shall not exceed the amount of unpaid debt, less any unearned interest or finance charges, plus an amount equal to two monthly payments.

    3.) Insurance on educational, agricultural, and horticultural credit commitments may be written on a level-term plan for the loan amount.

    4.) If the loan has a variable interest rate, the initial rate or the scheduled rates based on the initial index will be used in determining the loan amount, and subsequent changes to the variable interest rate will be disregarded.

b. Credit accident and health insurance

    1.) In the event of a disability, the total amount of debt payable by credit accident and health insurance shall not exceed the total of the scheduled unpaid loan installments; the amount of each periodic debt payment shall not exceed the original loan amount, divided by the number of periodic installments.

    2.) If the loan has a variable interest rate, the initial rate or the scheduled rates based on the initial index will be used in determining the loan amount, and subsequent changes to the variable interest rate will be disregarded.

    3.) If for any reason a policy of credit disability insurance does not provide coverage for the total amount of debt on a loan, or debt in the event of any one instance of disability, the applicant must be provided with a written disclosure on or accompanying the application. The disclosure must state that if the insured becomes disabled at a point where the number of monthly installment payments remaining exceeds the period of coverage provided by the policy, the benefits available will be less than the amount necessary to pay off the loan.

    4.) Unless specified in the policy, an insurer is not required to provide coverage for the final payment of a balloon loan, or for a period that exceeds the age limitation in the policy, or for amounts that exceed the insurer's maximum liability limits.

F. GROUP LIFE [61A.092; 62B.03] In a typical group life insurance plan, the employer offers and pays for an amount of annually renewable term life insurance equal to the employee's annual salary. This insurance usually does not require proof of insurability.

1. Continuation of Coverage [61A.092] In Minnesota, COBRA-like rules apply to group term life insurance. The employee is allowed to continue coverage through the group policy even after termination. In this situation, the employee, employer, and insurer all have certain responsibilities regarding notification and payment.

a. Every group life insurance policy issued in Minnesota must contain a provision that permits covered employees who are voluntarily or involuntarily terminated or laid off to continue the coverage for themselves and their dependents. An employee is considered to be laid off if there is a reduction in hours to the point where the employee is no longer eligible for coverage under the group life insurance policy. Termination does not include discharge for gross misconduct.

b. The covered employee is eligible to continue coverage for a period of 18 months after termination, or until obtaining coverage under another group policy, whichever is shorter. Employees electing to continue coverage must pay the monthly premium to their former employer; the premium charged may not exceed 102% of the plan cost.

c. Upon termination or layoff, the covered employee has 60 days within which to elect to continue coverage. The employer must provide written notice to the employee of the continuation options, which are:
- the employee's right to elect to continue coverage;
- the monthly amount the employee must pay to the employer to retain the coverage;
- when and where payment to the employer must be made; and
- the date payments are due to the employer.

d. If the employer fails to notify a covered employee of the options, the employer is still liable for the employee's coverage to the same extent the insurer would be if coverage were still in effect. The same responsibility applies if, after receiving timely payment from the employee, the employer fails to pay the insurer.

e. If the covered employee dies during the 60-day election period before deciding whether to continue or reject coverage continuation, the employee will be considered to have elected continuation of coverage. The beneficiary previously selected is then entitled to a death benefit equal to the amount of insurance that would have been continued, less any unpaid premium owed at the time of death.

2. **Conversion of Coverage [61A.092]** A group life insurance policy that provides the option for continuation of coverage after termination must also include a provision allowing a covered employee, surviving spouse, or dependent to obtain from the group insurer an individual life insurance policy providing the same or substantially similar benefits. The conversion will be at the employee's, spouse's or dependent's option and expense, does not require further evidence of insurability, and must be made without interruption of coverage.

G. **INSURANCE INTEREST ACT [60A.078-.0789]** Also known as the "Insurable Interest Act," this statute prohibits the solicitation of a life insurance policy for the purpose of selling the policy in the secondary market. It prohibits stranger-originated life insurance practices in the state of Minnesota.

1. **Insurable Interest Required** An individual may not obtain a policy on the life of another unless policy benefits are payable to the owner/beneficiary, or the personal

representatives of the insured's estate, or a person having, at policy issuance, an insurable interest in the individual insured.

a. **Insured's own life** An individual has an insurable interest in one's own life, and an individual may designate any person as the beneficiary, provided securing the policy does not violate this statute.

b. In regards to insurance on the life of another, insurable interest includes only the following interests.

    1.) An individual has an insurable interest in the life of another person to whom the individual is closely related by blood or law and in whom the individual has a substantial interest created by love and affection.

    2.) An individual has an insurable interest in the life of another person if the individual has a lawful and substantial interest in the continued life of the insured, rather than having an interest in the death of the insured.

    3.) An individual party to a contract for the sale or purchase of an interest in any business entity, but only for the purpose of carrying out the purpose and intent of the contract.

    4.) A trust, or trustee of a trust, when a life insurance policy is owned by the trust, provided the policy proceeds are primarily for the benefit of the trust beneficiaries and the trust is not directly or indirectly used to violate the Insurable Interest Act.

    5.) A guardian, trustee, or other fiduciary holding property for the insured, provided the policy proceeds are used primarily for the persons having an insurable interest in the insured's life, and the guardianship or fiduciary relationship is not directly or indirectly used to violate the Insurable Interest Act.

    6.) A trustee, sponsor, or custodian of assets held in any ERISA plan or other retirement or employee benefit plan has an insurable interest in the participant's life as long as the participant provides written consent prior to the insurance purchase. An employer, trustee, sponsor, or custodian may not take adverse action or retaliate against a participant who does not consent to insurance being issued on the participant's life.

    7.) A business entity has an insurable interest in the life of any owner, director, officer, partner, manager, or key person of the entity or its affiliate or subsidiary. The key person must provide written consent prior to the insurance purchase. The business entity, affiliate, or subsidiary may not take adverse action or retaliate against any key person who does not consent to insurance being issued on the person's life.

    8.) A financial institution or other person to whom a debt is owed, for the purposes of premium financing or otherwise, has an insurable interest in the life of the borrower. The insurable interest is limited to the amount of debt owed plus reasonable interest and service charges.

c. **Consent of insured** An individual life insurance policy is not effective unless the individual insured applies for or consents in writing to the policy and its terms. The insured must provide consent on or before the effective date; if the insured does not have the legal capacity to enter the contract, consent may be given by someone else in the following cases.

  1.) A parent or someone having legal custody of a minor may consent to a policy on a dependent child.

  2.) A court-appointed guardian may consent to a policy on the person under guardianship.

  3.) A court-appointed conservator of a person's estate may consent to a policy on the person whose estate is under conservatorship.

  4.) An attorney-in-fact may consent to a policy on the person who appointed the attorney-in-fact for the limited purpose of replacing a policy with a new policy, provided the aggregate amount of insurance remains the same or decreases.

  5.) A trustee of a revocable trust may consent to a policy on the life of the trust's settler.

  6.) A court of general jurisdiction may consent to a policy upon showing sufficient facts to justify issuing the policy.

2. Prohibited Practices

a. It is unlawful for any person to obtain or attempt to obtain a life insurance policy if one does not have an insurable interest in the insured's life. Insurable interest is defined in statute 60A.0783.

b. An individual may not engage in stranger-originated life insurance practices.

  1.) Stranger-originated life insurance practices (STOLI) STOLI is defined as initiating a life insurance policy for the benefit of a third-party investor who, at the time of policy origination, has no insurable interest in the insured. Trusts created to give the appearance of insurable interest and used to initiate policies for investors violate the insurable interest requirements and the prohibition against STOLI practices. STOLI practices include, but are not limited to:
  - purchasing life insurance with resources or guarantees from a person or entity, who, at the time of policy inception, could not lawfully initiate the policy themselves; and
  - at the time of inception agreeing to directly or indirectly transfer the ownership of the policy and/or the policy benefits to a third party.

c. An individual may not solicit, market, or promote the purchase of a policy for the purpose of selling the policy in the secondary market.

d. It is unlawful to enter into a premium finance agreement in which the lender receives proceeds, fees, or other consideration that are in addition to the amounts required to pay the principal, interest, and service charges related to policy premiums. Any payments, charges, fees, or other amounts in addition to the principal, interest, and service charges related to policy premiums, paid under the premium finance agreement, shall be remitted to the insured or to the insured's estate.

e. It is unlawful to enter into or offer to enter into a settlement contract prior to a policy being issued.

3. **Settlement Contracts** A prospective purchaser or beneficial interest in a policy may not, prior to issuance of a policy or during the first four years of the policy, enter into a settlement contract or any other agreement to acquire the policy or acquire a beneficial interest in the policy unless the prospective purchaser has determined the following through a reasonable inquiry.

   ■ Before issuing the policy there was no agreement or understanding between the insured, policyowner, or owner of a beneficial interest in the policy, and another person to guarantee any liability or to purchase the policy or an interest in the policy, including through an assumption or forgiveness of a loan.

   ■ Policy premiums are funded by the insured's personal assets or assets provided by a person who is closely related to the insured by blood or law or who has a lawful and substantial economic interest in the continued life of the insured.

   ■ The insured underwent a life expectancy evaluation within the 18-month time period immediately prior to policy issuance and, during the same time period, the evaluation results were not shared with or used by any person for the purpose of determining the actual or potential value of the policy in the secondary market. A life expectancy evaluation can be shared with or used by the insured or the insured's accountant, attorney, or insurance producer for estate planning purposes as long as the evaluation is not used by those individuals to determine the actual or potential value of the policy in the secondary market.

   a. Legitimate insurance transactions The statute does not prevent a policyholder from entering into a legitimate settlement contract, nor does it prevent any person from soliciting a person to enter into a legitimate settlement contract. It does not prevent the assignment, sale, transfer, or bequest of the death benefit or policy ownership, provided those actions are associated with a legitimate settlement contract and not part of STOLI practices.

   b. Certification The prospective purchaser has a requirement to request certification from the settlement broker that any life expectancy evaluation performed on the insured prior to the policy issuance was not used by or shared with any other person prior to the policy issuance for the purpose of determining the actual or potential value of the policy in the secondary market.

4. **Presumption of STOLI Practices** A settlement contract or any agreement to sell or acquire the policy or beneficial interest in the policy, entered into within the first four years of the policy, is presumed to be a STOLI practice if either of the following circumstances is present.

   a. Before issuing the policy there was an agreement or understanding between the insured, policyowner, or owner of a beneficial interest in the policy and another person to guarantee any liability or to purchase the policy or an interest in the policy, including through an assumption or forgiveness of a loan.

   b. Both of the following are present.
      ■ Policy premiums are funded by means other than the insured's personal assets or assets provided by a person who is closely related to the insured by blood or law or who has a lawful and substantial economic interest in the continued life of the insured. Funds from a premium finance loan are considered assets of the insured only if the insured or that person is contractually obligated to repay the full amount of the loan and to pledge personal assets, other than the policy itself, for loan amounts exceeding the policy's cash value.
      ■ The insured underwent a life expectancy evaluation within the 18-month time period immediately prior to policy issuance and, during the same time period, the evaluation results were shared with or used by any person for the purpose of determining the actual or potential value of the policy in the secondary market.

5. **Change of Ownership or Beneficiary Requests** When an insurer receives a properly completed request for change of ownership or beneficiary the insurer must respond in writing within 30 calendar days confirming the change has been made or indicating why the requested change cannot be processed. The insurer shall not unreasonably delay the change of ownership or beneficiary request and shall not interfere with any permitted settlement contract entered into in this state. The insurer's ability to make other inquires to detect STOLI practices is not limited by this section.

   a. **Written questionnaire** If the insurer receives a request for change of ownership or beneficiary within the first four years of the policy, the insurer may require the policyowner to complete and return a written questionnaire. The questionnaire is designed to determine whether the change request relates to a settlement contract and if so, whether STOLI practices are present. The questionnaire must be approved by the Commissioner and shall include the following:
      ■ The definition of settlement contract
      ■ An inquiry regarding whether the request for change of ownership or beneficiary relates to or is made in accordance with a settlement contract
      ■ If the request relates to a settlement contract, an inquiry regarding whether STOLI practices are present
      ■ A disclosure that presenting false material information, or concealing material information in connection with the questionnaire is defined under Minnesota law as a fraudulent act

■ A signed certification by the policyowner that the answers and information provided in the questionnaire are true and complete to the best of the policyowner's knowledge and belief

b. **Fraternal benefit societies** The Insurable Interest Act does not prohibit a fraternal benefit society regulated under Minnesota statute from enforcing the terms of its bylaws or rules regarding permitted beneficiaries and owners.

6. **Fraudulent Acts** Any person who commits a fraudulent act, or permits any of its employees or agents to commit a fraudulent act, may be punished via fine, imprisonment, and restitution. All of the following acts are fraudulent when committed with the intent to defraud and for the purpose of monetary gain or depriving another of property:

■ When asked, failing to disclose to the insurer that the prospective insured has undergone a life expectancy evaluation

■ Misrepresenting a person's state of residence or facilitating the change of a person's state of residence for the purpose of evading or avoiding the provisions of the Insurable Interest Act

■ Presenting or preparing false material information, or concealing any material information related to a written questionnaire or other documents or communications designed to detect STOLI practices or comply with the Insurable Interest Act

■ Encouraging the insured, policyowner, or owner of a beneficial interest in the policy to falsely state that STOLI practices are not present; or aiding in the preparation or execution of documents designed to create the false impression that those circumstances are not present

■ Failing to request or provide the broker certification required by law, or falsely certifying that the life expectancy evaluation was not shared with any other person prior to the policy issuance for the purpose of determining the actual or potential value of the policy in the secondary market

7. **Actions to Recover Death Benefits [60A.0789]**

a. If the beneficiary, assignee, or other payee receives the death benefits under a life insurance policy initiated by STOLI practices or secured in violation of the insurable interest or settlement contract requirements, the personal representative of the insured's estate or other lawfully acting agent may take action to recover such benefits from the person receiving them.

b. If a person receives the death benefit as a result of a nonwillful violation of the Insurable Interest Act, the court may limit the recovery to unjust enrichment, calculated as the benefits received plus interest from the date of receipt, less premiums paid by the recipient and any consideration paid by the recipient to the insured in connection with the policy.

c. If a person receives the death benefit as the result of a willful violation of the Insurable Interest Act, the court may, in addition to actual damages, order the defendant(s) to pay exemplary damages in an amount up to two times the death benefits. A pattern of violations of the Insurable Interest Act and conduct involving one or more fraudulent acts are evidence of willfulness. The exemplary damages shall be paid to one or more governmental agencies that combats consumer fraud, including the Department of Commerce.

d. The court may award reasonable attorney fees, together with costs and disbursements, to any party that recovers damages in any action brought about by this section of the Insurable Interest Act.

e. Any action to recover death benefits must be brought within two years after the death of the insured.

f. Any contract, agreement, arrangement, or transaction prohibited by the Insurable Interest Act is voidable.

g. Prior to paying death benefits, if the insurer believes the policy was initiated by STOLI practices, the insurer may bring a declaratory judgment action seeking a court order declaring the policy void.

h. The Insurable Interest Act does not limit other civil remedies; prohibit other law enforcement or regulatory agencies from investigating suspected violations of the law; limit the powers of the commissioner or insurance fraud unit to investigate possible violations of the law; or limit the power of the state of Minnesota to expend punishment for crimes committed under other laws of the state.

H. REPLACEMENT INSURANCE [61A.53-.60] This statute addresses the duties of insurers, agents and brokers regarding the replacement of a life insurance policy or an annuity. A "replacement" sale is defined as an action using current insurance values to purchase new coverage either with the same insurer or another insurer. The client may be vulnerable to producer "churning"—unnecessary changes or replacements that are more for the producer's benefit than the insured's. Caution must be used in replacing life insurance in particular because the insured's age has increased, and their health status may have changed since the original date of purchase. It also addresses "conservation" which is any attempt by the existing insurer or its agent or broker to dissuade a policyowner or contract holder from the replacement of an existing life insurance or annuity.

1. Duties of Agents and Brokers

a. Submission to insurer Each agent or broker who initiates the application will submit the following with each life insurance or annuity application:

1.) A statement signed by the applicant as to whether replacement of an existing life insurance or annuity is involved in the transaction

2.) A signed statement as to whether the agent or broker knows replacement is involved in the transaction

b. Replacement information If replacement is involved, the agent or broker will:

- present to the applicant, no later than when the application is taken, a "Notice Regarding Replacement" on a form approved by the Commissioner. The notice will be fully completed and signed by both the applicant and the agent or broker and left with the applicant. The completed notice must list all existing life insurance and annuities to be replaced, properly identified by name of insurer, the insured, and contract number. If a contract number has not been assigned by the existing insurer, alternative identification, such as an application or receipt number, shall be listed;

- leave with the applicant the original or a copy of any written or printed communications used for presentation to the applicant; and

- submit to the replacing insurer with the application a copy of the fully completed and signed replacement notice provided under this subdivision.

c. Materials used to dissuade replacement Each agent or broker who uses written or printed communications in a conservation shall leave with the applicant the original or a copy of the communications.

2. Duties of All Insurers Each insurer shall inform its personnel responsible procedures for compliance with the replacement insurance statute of the statute requirements. The insurer must require with each completed life insurance or annuity application a statement signed by the applicant as to whether the proposed insurance or annuity replaces existing life insurance or annuities.

3. Duties of Insurers that Use Agents and Brokers

a. Each insurer that uses an agent or broker in a life insurance or annuity sale will require with each completed application a statement signed by the agent or broker as to whether she knows replacement is involved in the transaction.

b. When replacement is involved the insurer shall:

- require from the agent or broker with the application for life insurance or annuity, a copy of the fully completed and signed replacement notice provided to the applicant. The existing life insurance or annuity must be identified by name of insurer, insured, and contract number. If a number has not been assigned by the existing insurer, alternative identification, such as an application or receipt number, must be listed; and

- send to each existing insurer a written communication advising of the replacement or proposed replacement and the identification information. This written communication must be made within five working days of the date that the application is received in the replacing insurer's home or regional office, or the date the proposed policy or contract is issued, whichever is sooner.

c. The replacing insurer will maintain evidence of the "Notice Regarding Replacement" and a replacement register, cross-indexed, by replacing agent/broker and existing insurer to be replaced. Evidence that all requirements were met must be maintained for at least six years.

d. The replacing insurer will provide in its policy or contract, or in a separate written notice delivered with the policy or contract, that the applicant has a right to an unconditional refund of all premiums paid. This right may be exercised within a period of 30 days beginning from the date of delivery of the policy.

4. Duties of Insurers With Respect to Direct Response Sales

a. When soliciting a direct response sale, if a replacement is involved and the insurer did not propose the replacement, the insurer will send a Commissioner-approved replacement notice to the applicant; the notice must accompany the policy or contract.

b. If the insurer proposed the replacement, the insurer will:
- provide to applicants or prospective applicants a replacement notice approved by the Commissioner; the notice shall accompany the application;
- request from the applicant a list of all existing life insurance policies or annuity contracts to be replaced, properly identified by name of insurer and insured;
- send to each existing insurer a written communication advising of the replacement or proposed replacement and the identification information. The written communication must be made within five working days of the date that the application is received in the replacing insurer's home or regional office, or the date the proposed policy or contract is issued, whichever is sooner;
- maintain evidence of the "Notice Regarding Replacement" and a replacement register. Evidence that all requirements were met must be maintained for at least six years; and
- provide in its policy or contract, or in a separate written notice delivered with the policy or contract, that the applicant has a right to an unconditional refund of all premiums paid. This right may be exercised within a period of 30 days beginning from the date of delivery of the policy.

5. **Enforcement and Compliance** An agent, broker, or insurer shall not recommend the replacement or conservation of an existing policy or contract by using a substantially inaccurate presentation or comparison of an existing policy's or contract's premiums, benefits, dividends, or values. An insurer, agent, representative, officer, or employee of the insurer failing to comply with the requirements of this section is subject to penalty.

a. Patterns of action by policyholders or contract holders who purchase replacing policies or contracts from the same agent or broker, after indicating on applications that replacement is not involved, are assumed to be evidence of the agent's or broker's knowledge that replacement was intended in connection with the sale of those policies. Such patterns of action are evidence of the agent's or broker's intent to violate this statute.

b. Even if an insurer, agent, or broker complies with sections of this statute the insured may still take action or seek other remedies against an insurer, agent, or broker. In a proceeding in which the insured's knowledge or understanding is an issue, compliance with those sections may be admitted as evidence, but shall not be conclusive.

6. Exemptions

a. Unless otherwise specifically included, sections of this statute affecting replacement insurance do not apply to transactions involving:

- credit life insurance;

- group life insurance or group annuities;

- an application to the existing insurer that issued the existing life insurance or annuity, where a contractual change or conversion privilege is being exercised;

- proposed life insurance that is replacing life insurance under a binding or conditional receipt issued by the same company; or

- transactions where the replacing insurer and the existing insurer are the same, or are subsidiaries or affiliates under common ownership or control. Agents or brokers proposing replacement must still submit to the insurer with the application

  — a statement signed by the applicant as to whether replacement of existing life insurance or annuity is involved in the transaction; and

  — a signed statement as to whether the agent or broker knows replacement is involved in the transaction.

III. MINNESOTA LAWS, RULES, AND REGULATIONS PERTINENT TO HEALTH INSURANCE ONLY

A. POLICY CLAUSES AND PROVISIONS/MANDATES

1. Coverage of Emotionally Handicapped Children [62A.151] All health, medical, hospitalization, and accident and sickness insurance policies, including nonprofit health service plans, and health maintenance organizations (HMO), which provide coverage for inpatient hospital and medical expenses, must provide benefits for the treatment of emotionally disabled children in a residential treatment facility. The requirements do not apply to any plan or policy that is individually underwritten, or provided for a specific individual and family members as a nongroup policy. The mandatory coverage shall be on the same basis as inpatient hospital coverage provided under the policy.

2. Coverage of Disabled Children [62A.14, .141]

a. All group health insurance policies, including nonprofit health service plans, and health maintenance organizations (HMO), must cover disabled dependents of the insured, subscriber, or enrollee of the policy or plan. The policy or plan may not contain any provision concerning limitations on preexisting conditions, insurability, eligibility, or health underwriting approval for disabled dependents.

b. Coverage through an individual or group health policy for dependent children may not be terminated while the child is and continues to be both 1) incapable of self-sustaining employment by reason of developmental disability, mental illness or disorder, or physical disability; and 2) chiefly dependent upon the policyholder for support and maintenance. Proof of the incapacity and dependency must be furnished to the insurer, HMO, or organization within 31 days of the child reaching the policy's limiting age and annually two years after the limiting age was attained.

3. Coverage of Newborns and Adopted Children [62A.27, 62A.042]

a. All individual and group health insurance and health maintenance contracts must cover a newborn infant immediately from the moment of birth for illness, injury, congenital malformation, or premature birth. Newborn infants include grandchildren who are financially dependent upon a covered grandparent and who reside with the grandparent continuously from birth. Notification to a health carrier is not required to receive this coverage. However, the health carrier is entitled to all additional premiums due.

b. The coverage for newborns includes benefits for medical and dental treatment up to the limiting age for dependent coverage. This includes orthodontic and oral surgery treatment to correct a cleft lip or cleft palate. Benefits for individuals age 19 up to the limiting age for dependent coverage are limited to medical and dental treatment that was scheduled or initiated prior to the dependent turning age 19. If orthodontic services are eligible for coverage under a dental insurance plan, that plan is primary. Payment for dental or orthodontic treatment not related to the congenital condition of cleft lip or cleft palate is not covered.

c. A health plan that provides coverage to a Minnesota resident must cover adopted children of the insured, subscriber, participant or enrollee on the same basis as other dependents. The plan may not contain any provision concerning limitations on preexisting conditions, insurability, eligibility, or health underwriting approval for children placed for adoption with the participant. The coverage is effective as of the date of placement for adoption. Notification to a health carrier is not required in order to receive this coverage. However, the health carrier is entitled to all additional premiums due.

4. Continuation/Conversion of Benefits [62A.17, 62A.21, 62A.65, 62D.101, 62A.145-.148]

a. Guaranteed renewal [62A.65] No individual health plan may be offered, sold, issued, or renewed to a Minnesota resident unless the health plan provides that the plan is guaranteed renewable at a premium rate that does not take into account the claims experience or any change in the health status of any covered person that occurred after the initial issuance of the health plan to the person. The premium rate upon renewal must also otherwise comply with this section. A health carrier must not refuse to renew an individual health plan, except for nonpayment of premiums, fraud, or misrepresentation.

Also, an individual policy or contract issued as a conversion policy prior to January 1, 2014, will be renewable at the option of the covered person as long as the covered person is not covered under another qualified plan.

b. **Disabled Employees** If an employee becomes totally disabled and misses work because of the total disability, neither the employer nor the employer's insurer can terminate, suspend, or restrict group insurance benefits solely because of the employee's absence. This includes coverage for the employee's dependents. If the employee is required to pay the premium for the coverage extension, payment shall be made to the employer.

c. **Survivors** No accident and health insurance policy issued by an insurer, nonprofit health service plan corporation, or health maintenance organization (HMO), that provides coverage for dependents shall, except upon the written consent of the survivor(s), terminate, suspend, or otherwise restrict benefits to the survivor(s) until the earlier of the following dates:

   ■ The date the surviving spouse becomes covered under another group health plan

   ■ The date coverage would have terminated under the policy had the insured lived

   1.) The survivor(s) may be required to pay the entire monthly premium. The policy, contract, or plan must require the group policyholder or contract holder to provide the insured with written verification of the coverage cost promptly at the time of eligibility and at any time during the continuation period.

   2.) At no time shall the premium or fee contributions charged exceed 102% of the plan cost.

   3.) If the survivor fails to make premium or fee payments within 90 days after payment notification, the insurer may terminate coverage without written consent. If the coverage is terminated for non-payment, written notice of cancellation must be mailed to the survivor's last known address at least 30 days before the cancellation.

   4.) If the coverage is provided under a group policy, contract, or plan, then the survivor shall make the premium payments to the group policyholder or contract holder for remittance to the insurer, nonprofit health service plan corporation, or HMO.

   5.) *Survivor* means a person who would be entitled to, and dependent upon, economic support by an insured, subscriber, or enrollee if that person were alive; this includes a spouse, child, or children as defined by the accident and health policy.

d. **Termination of Employment** Every group insurance policy, group subscriber contract, and health care plan covering a Minnesota resident employed in this state must contain a provision that permits covered employees who are voluntarily or involuntarily terminated or laid off to continue the coverage for themselves and their dependents.

1.) An employee is considered to be laid off if there is a reduction in hours to the point where the employee is no longer eligible for coverage under the policy, contract, or health care plan. Termination does not include discharge for gross misconduct.

2.) The employee is eligible to continue coverage for a period of 18 months after termination, or until obtaining coverage under another group health plan, whichever is shorter. If the employee becomes covered under another group policy, contract, or health plan that contains limitations for preexisting conditions, the employee may, subject to the 18-month maximum continuation limit, continue coverage with the former employer until the preexisting condition limitations have been satisfied. The new policy or health plan is primary except as to the preexisting condition. In the case of a newborn child who is a dependent of the employee, the new policy is primary upon the birth of the child, regardless of which coverage is primary for the child's mother.

3.) Employees electing to continue coverage must pay the monthly premium to their former employer; the premium charged may not exceed 102% of the plan cost. The policy, contract, or plan must require the group policyholder or contract holder to provide the insured with written verification of the coverage cost promptly at the time of eligibility and at any time during the continuation period. Upon request by the terminated or laid off employee, a health carrier must provide the necessary instructions to enable the employee to elect continuation of coverage.

4.) Upon termination or layoff the employee has 60 days to decide if they want to continue coverage. The employer must provide written notice to the employee of the continuation options, which are:
- the employee's right to elect to continue coverage;
- the monthly amount the employee must pay to the employer to retain the coverage;
- when and where payment to the employer must be made; and
- the date payments are due to the employer.

5.) If the employer fails to notify a covered employee of the continuation options, the employer is still liable for the employee's coverage to the same extent the insurer would be liable if coverage were still in effect. The same responsibility applies if, after receiving timely payment from the employee, the employer fails to pay the insurer, nonprofit health service plan corporation, or HMO.

6.) A group insurance policy that provides the option for continuation of coverage after termination must also include a provision allowing a covered employee, surviving spouse, or dependent to obtain from the group insurer an individual insurance policy providing at least the minimum benefits of a qualified plan. The conversion will be at the employee's, spouse's or dependent's option and expense, does not require further evidence of insurability, and must be made without interruption of coverage. The application and premium payment must be made to the insurer within 30 days following notice of the expiration of the continued coverage.

e. Divorce [62A.21] No accident and health insurance policy or health maintenance contract that provides coverage for the insured's spouse shall contain a provision for termination of coverage for the spouse solely as a result of divorce. Every policy or health maintenance contract shall contain a provision that permits continuation of coverage for the insured's former spouse and dependent children upon furnishing a divorce decree. The coverage shall be renewed and continued until the earlier of the following dates:

■ The date the insured's former spouse becomes covered under any other group health plan or Medicare

■ The date coverage would otherwise terminate under the policy or health maintenance contract

1.) If coverage is provided under a group policy, any required premium will be paid by the insured on a monthly basis to the group policyholder who will remit the payment to the insurer or HMO. The policy must require the group policyholder to provide the insured with written verification of the coverage cost promptly at the time of eligibility and at any time during the continuation period.

2.) At no time shall the premium charged exceed 102% of the plan cost. Upon request by the insured's former spouse or dependent child, a health carrier must provide the necessary instructions to enable the spouse or dependent to elect continuation of coverage.

3.) Every policy or health maintenance contract shall contain a provision allowing the insured's former spouse and dependent children, without providing evidence of insurability, to obtain conversion coverage from the insurer or HMO. The conversion coverage will be effective at the expiration of any continuation of coverage and will provide at least the minimum benefits of a qualified plan. The application and premium payment must be made to the insurer within 30 days following notice of the expiration of the continued coverage.

1.) Effective January 1, 2014, an individual policy or contract issued as a conversion policy prior to January 1, 2014, will be renewable at the option of the covered person as long as the covered person is not covered under another qualified plan. Any revisions in the table of rate for the individual policy will apply to the insured's original age at entry and apply equally to all similar conversion policies.

5. Benefits for Treatment of Mental Health and Chemical Dependency [62Q.47]

a. Whether in- or outpatient, cost-sharing requirements and benefit or service limitations for hospital mental health and hospital and residential chemical dependency and alcoholism services must not place a greater financial burden on the insured or enrollee, or be more restrictive than those requirements and limitations for similar hospital medical services not related to an alcohol or chemical dependency. All health plans must meet the requirements of the Affordable Care Act concerning these patients.

6. **Standard Provisions [62A.04]** Each accident and health policy delivered or issued to a Minnesota resident must contain the following **required provisions** and use approved language unless reapproved by the Commissioner:

   a. **Entire contract** The entire contract is the policy itself and any endorsements and attached papers. Only the insurer may approve changes, which must be attached to the policy. No agent has authority to change the policy or to waive any of its provisions.

   b. **Time limit on certain defenses** After two years from the policy issue date, no misstatements made by the applicant, except fraudulent misstatements, shall be used to void the policy or deny a claim. After the policy has been in force for a period of two years during the lifetime of the insured (excluding any period during which the insured is disabled), it shall become incontestable as to the statements contained in the application. No claim commencing after two years from the policy's issue date shall be reduced or denied on the ground that it was a pre-existing condition.

   c. **Grace period** A grace period of seven days for weekly premium policies, 10 days for monthly premium policies, and 31 days for all other policies will be allowed for the payment of each premium. The grace period does not apply to the first premium due. After January 1, 2014, grace period will include the following additional phrase.

      ◼ For qualified health plans sold through the Minnesota insurance marketplace to individuals receiving advance payments of the premium tax credit, a grace period provision must be included that complies with the Affordable Care Act and is no less restrictive than the grace period required by the Affordable Care Act.

   d. **Reinstatement** If the insured wishes to reinstate a lapsed policy, the insurer may require a reinstatement application and proof of insurability. If the insurer does not require a reinstatement application, the insured is automatically covered when their premiums have been collected. The insurer may collect no more than 60 days of past due premiums with the reinstatement application, and will issue a conditional receipt. The insured is automatically covered if the insurer has not rejected their reinstatement application within 45 days. Coverage for accidental injury begins immediately upon reinstatement; loss due to sickness is subject to a 10-day waiting period.

   e. **Notice of claim** Written notice of a medical claim must be given to the insurer within 20 days after the loss, or as soon thereafter as is reasonably possible. If the claim is for disability benefits, the insured shall, every six months after the original claim notice, provide the insurer with notice of the continued disability, except in the event of legal incapacity.

f. **Claim forms** The insurer must send its claim forms to the claimant within 15 days after receiving notice of a claim. If the forms are not furnished within the required time frame the claimant may submit written proof of the loss and shall be deemed to have complied with the requirements.

g. **Proof of loss** Written proof of loss must be furnished to the insurer within 90 days after the date of loss. Failure to furnish proof within 90 days will not invalidate or reduce any claim if it was not reasonably possible to give proof within that time. In that case, proof of loss must be furnished as soon as reasonably possible, and except in the absence of legal capacity, no later than one year from the time it was required.

h. **Time payment of claims** Medical claims will be paid immediately upon receipt of written proof of loss. Disability claims will be paid at least monthly.

i. **Payment of claims** Benefits for loss of life will be payable in accordance with the beneficiary designation and policy provisions effective at the time of payment. If no beneficiary is designated, benefits shall be payable to the insured's estate. All other benefits will be paid to the insured.

j. **Physical examinations and autopsy** The insurer may require physical exams of the insured when and as often as it may reasonably require during the claim, and may also conduct an autopsy in case of death. Both are paid by the insurer.

k. **Legal actions** The insured must wait at least 60 days after furnishing written proof of loss to take legal action against the insurer to collect benefits. No legal action can be brought after three years from the time written proof of loss is required.

l. **Change of beneficiary** Only the owner/insured may change the beneficiary; the beneficiary's consent is not required to assign or make changes to the policy, or change the beneficiary.

7. **Optional Provisions** Each accident and health policy delivered or issued to a Minnesota resident may contain the following **optional provisions:**

a. **Change of occupation** If the insured changes to a more hazardous occupation, the insurer will pay only the portion of benefits that the premiums paid would have purchased at the rates for the more hazardous occupation. If the insured changes to a less hazardous occupation, the insurer will reduce the premiums and will return the excess pro rata unearned premium. The insured must provide proof of the occupational change.

b. **Misstatement of age** If the age of the insured has been misstated, all amounts payable under the policy will be adjusted to what the premium paid would have purchased at the correct age.

c. **Other insurance with the same insurer** If the insured has two like policies with the same insurer in force at the same time, the excess policy is cancelled and the premiums are refunded; benefits are paid out of the policy that is kept in force. The insured may choose which policy to keep in force.

d. **Insurance with other insurers** This provision applies to *expense incurred benefits*. If the insured has other valid coverage with another insurer providing benefits for the same loss, each insurer will pay a pro rata share of the covered loss.

e. **Insurance with other insurers** This provision applies to *other benefits*. If the insured has other valid coverage with another insurer providing benefits for the same loss, each insurer will pay a pro rata share of the covered loss.

f. **Relation of earnings to insurance** If the total monthly loss of time (disability) benefits under all coverage in force exceeds the monthly earnings of the insured at the time of disability, the insurer is liable only for the proportionate amount of benefits based on the ratio of the insured's monthly earnings to the total amount of monthly benefits under all policies. Excess premiums shall be returned to the insured.

g. **Unpaid premium** Upon the payment of a claim under the policy, any premium due and unpaid may be deducted.

h. **Cancellation** The insurer may cancel a cancelable policy at any time with at least five days written notice delivered to the insured or mailed to the insured's last known address. The insurer will promptly return the unearned portion of premium paid, calculated on a pro rata basis. Policy cancellation will not affect any claim that originated prior to the cancellation date.

i. **Conformity with state statutes** Any provision of the policy that conflicts with the statutes of the state in which the insured resides is amended to conform to the minimum requirements of those statutes.

j. **Illegal occupation** The insurer shall not be liable for any loss if the insured was injured while committing a felony or if engaged in an illegal occupation.

k. **Narcotics** The insurer shall not be liable for any loss sustained or contracted if the insured was under the influence of any narcotic, unless administered on the advice of a physician.

B. **COMPREHENSIVE HEALTH INSURANCE ACT (CHIA) [62E]** This act established an insurance *safety net* for individuals who have been turned down for individual health insurance due to pre-existing conditions. Starting in 2014, the Commissioner of Commerce and the Minnesota Comprehensive Health Association will ensure that applicants for coverage through the federal qualified high-risk pool, or through the MCHA, are referred to the medical assistance or MinnesotaCare programs if they are potentially eligible for coverage through those programs. The commissioner of human services shall ensure that applicants who are not eligible for those programs are provided information about coverage through the federal qualified high-risk pool and the Minnesota Comprehensive Health Association.

[Minnesota will coordinate its efforts with the United States Department of Health and Human Services (HHS) to obtain the federal funds to implement in Minnesota the federal qualified high-risk pool.]

1. **Minnesota Comprehensive Health Association (MCHA) [2013, HF 779, art. 1, s 40, eff. 5-25-2013]** MCHA was established to offer individual health insurance policies to Minnesota residents who have been turned down for health insurance by the private market. MCHA is sometimes referred to as Minnesota's *high risk pool* for health insurance or *health insurance of last resort*. Premiums charged to policyholders are generally higher than rates for comparable policies in the marketplace. By law, MCHA premiums must be set between 101% and 125% of the average for comparable policies. For calendar years beginning January 1, 2014, and thereafter, premium rates shall be determined annually and effective January 1 of each year.

   a. The comprehensive health insurance plan is open for enrollment by eligible persons who must submit a written application. The application must include evidence of rejection, a requirement of restrictive riders, a rate up, or a preexisting conditions limitation on a qualified plan.

   b. No one who obtains coverage through the plan shall be covered for any preexisting condition during the first six months of coverage if the person was diagnosed or treated for the condition during the 90 days immediately preceding the date the application was received.

   c. MCHA offers various individual plan options, with annual calendar year deductibles ranging from $500 to $10,000; out-of-pocket expense maximums ranging from $3,000 to $10,000; and a $5,000,000 maximum lifetime benefit. Included in the offering are a High Deductible Health Plan and a Basic Medicare Supplement Plan.

   d. The plan does not provide coverage:
      - for injuries received in the course of employment and subject to workers' compensation law;
      - for injuries received in a motor vehicle accident for which benefits are payable under no-fault coverage; or
      - if benefits are payable under another accident and health insurance policy, Medicare, or another government program.

C. MEDICARE SUPPLEMENT PLANS [62A.31-.44] Medicare supplement policies are sold by private sector insurance companies to enhance, expand, and also fill in many of the gaps left by Medicare. Senior citizens may purchase an individual or group supplement policy. Minnesota law currently establishes minimum standards for two types of supplement policies: Basic and Extended Basic.

1. **Minimum standards** Insurers and producers are bound by several statutes related to Medicare supplement coverage, advertising, and the actual sale itself.

   a. **Preexisting condition coverage** The policy must cover preexisting conditions during the first six months of coverage if the insured was not diagnosed or treated for the particular condition during the 90 days immediately preceding the effective date of coverage.

   b. **Limitation on cancellation or nonrenewal** The policy must contain a provision that the plan will not be cancelled or nonrenewed on the grounds of the deterioration of the insured's health.

   c. **Mandatory offer** Before the policy is sold or issued, an offer of both categories of Medicare supplement insurance must be made to the individual, along with an explanation of both coverages. A written notification must be given stating that counseling services may be available to provide advice concerning the purchase of Medicare supplement policies and enrollment under the Medicaid program.

   d. **Outline of coverage** An outline of coverage must be delivered at the time of application and prior to premium payment, and an acknowledgment of receipt of the outline must be obtained from the applicant.

   e. **Guaranteed renewability** The policy must guarantee renewability. No issuer of Medicare supplement insurance policies may cancel or nonrenew a policy or certificate for any reason other than nonpayment of premium or material misrepresentation.

   f. **Each policy must specify whether it** is an extended basic Medicare supplement plan or a basic Medicare supplement plan, and must note that the extended basic Medicare supplement is the more comprehensive of the two policies.

2. **Suspension for medical assistance** Policyholders are able to suspend coverage in the event they are entitled to medical assistance.

   a. At the request of the policyholder, benefits and premiums can be suspended for up to 24 months while the policyholder is entitled to medical assistance. The policyholder must notify the supplement policy issuer within 90 days after the date the individual becomes entitled to medical assistance.

   b. If suspension occurs and if the policyholder loses entitlement to medical assistance, the policy shall automatically be reinstated, effective the date of termination of medical assistance. The policyholder must provide notice of loss of medical assistance within 90 days after the date of the loss and pay the premium for that period.

c. Upon reinstatement, there is no additional waiting period for treatment of preexisting conditions, and coverage must be substantially equivalent to the coverage in effect before the date of the suspension.

3. **Replacement coverage** If a Medicare supplement policy replaces another supplement, the issuer of the replacing policy shall waive any time periods related to preexisting conditions, waiting periods, elimination periods, and probationary periods in the new Medicare supplement policy.

4. **Requirements**

   a. **Advertising** The Commissioner will review and approve any Medicare supplement advertisement, whether in printed or electronic form, intended for use in Minnesota.

   b. **Free-look period** Policyholders have the right to return the Medicare supplement policy within 30 days of its delivery if, after reviewing the policy, the insured is not satisfied for any reason. This notice must be prominently printed on the first page of the policy; the insurer will provide a full refund upon return of the policy.

   c. Commissions paid to licensed producers for the sale of Medicare supplement policies must be level for the first four years.

   d. **Replacement requirements** An insurer or agent may replace a Medicare supplement plan only under the following circumstances.

      1.) There is an upgrade in coverage.

      2.) The insured has demonstrated dissatisfaction with their current insurer.

      3.) There is an exact replacement of coverage and a substantial cost savings. An insurer or agent may replace a Medicare supplement plan with a less-comprehensive plan only if the prospective insured signs an acknowledgment that they will receive less benefits under the replacement policy than the current policy.

5. **Prohibited acts** A Medicare supplement policy or certificate may not duplicate benefits already provided by Medicare, or contain coverage exclusions that are more restrictive than those of Medicare. The supplement may not use waivers to exclude, limit, or reduce coverage or benefits for specifically named preexisting diseases or physical conditions, unless permitted by the preexisting coverage conditions.

   a. **Government endorsements** Policies and promotional literature may not display a seal or emblem implying there is a connection, certification, approval or endorsement from Medicare or any governmental body of Minnesota.

    b. An insurer or producer may not sell a Medicare supplement to someone who does not already have Medicare Part A and B.

    c. An insurer or producer may not sell more than one Medicare supplement to a person.

6. Disclosures All individual or group Medicare supplement plans delivered or issued in Minnesota are required to show the type of plan on the cover. In addition, an outline containing the following information must be delivered to the applicant at the time of application.

    a. A description of the principal benefits and coverage provided in the policy.

    b. A statement of the exceptions, reductions, and limitations contained in the policy including the following language in bold print: "**THIS POLICY DOES NOT COVER ALL MEDICAL EXPENSES BEYOND THOSE COVERED BY MEDICARE. THIS POLICY DOES NOT COVER ALL SKILLED NURSING HOME CARE EXPENSES AND DOES NOT COVER CUSTODIAL OR RESIDENTIAL NURSING CARE. READ YOUR POLICY CAREFULLY TO DETERMINE WHICH NURSING HOME FACILITIES AND EXPENSES ARE COVERED BY YOUR POLICY.**"

    c. A statement of the renewal provisions, including the insurer's right to change premiums. The premium and how it must be paid should be stated, along with premium illustrations.

    d. A statement that the outline of coverage is a summary and the policy should be read very carefully for specific provisions. Additionally, the policy does not provide all details of Medicare coverage; the policyholder should contact the Social Security office or consult the Medicare handbook for more details.

    e. A statement of the policy's loss ratio, which is how much of every $100 in premium will be returned as benefits to policyholders over the life of the contract.

    f. If the outline of coverage has changed since the time of application, a substitute outline will accompany the policy when delivered with the following notice: "NOTICE: Read this outline of coverage carefully. It is not identical to the outline of coverage provided upon application, and the coverage originally applied for has not been issued."

    g. The policyholder has the right to return the policy or certificate for a full refund. The policy will contain the following language regarding the free look period: "If you find that you are not satisfied with your policy or certificate for any reason, you may return it to the insurer. If you send the policy or certificate back to us within 30 days after you receive it, we will treat the policy as if it had never been issued and return all of your payments within 10 days."

h. A statement regarding policy or certificate replacement must be visible. "If you are replacing another health insurance policy or certificate, do NOT cancel it until you have actually received your new policy or certificate and are sure you want to keep it."

i. A statement will advise purchasers that the policy or certificate may not fully cover all medical costs, and that neither the insurer nor its agents are connected with Medicare.

j. A statement advising the applicant to answer all medical and health history questions truthfully and completely; to review the application carefully before signing; and that the insurer may cancel the policy and refuse to pay any claims if information is omitted, or if the applicant has falsified medical information (unless the policy is guaranteed issue).

7. Penalties Any insurer or producer who violates any of the laws applying to the solicitation and sale of Medicare supplement plans is guilty of a felony, and is subject to a civil penalty of not more than $5,000 per violation. The Commissioner may also revoke or suspend the insurer or producer's license. An agent or producer who violates the laws applying to selling replacement policies, selling duplicate policies, and selling without a license is guilty of a felony and subject to a civil penalty of not more than $5,000 per violation.

8. Basic Medicare Supplement Plan

a. Coverage The basic supplement plan must have a level of coverage that will provide:

- coverage for Medicare Part A coinsurance amounts, and 100% of all Part A eligible hospitalization expenses not covered by Medicare, after satisfying the Part A deductible;

- coverage for the daily co-payment amount of Part A eligible expenses for the calendar year incurred for skilled nursing facility care;

- coverage for the coinsurance amount or, where applicable, the co-payment amount of Medicare eligible expenses under Part B, subject to the Medicare Part B deductible amount;

- 80% of the hospital and medical expenses and supplies incurred during travel outside the United States as a result of a medical emergency;

- coverage for the reasonable cost of the first three pints of blood, or equivalent quantities of packed red blood cells; applies to Part A or Part B;

- 100% of the cost of immunizations not otherwise covered under Part D and routine screening procedures for cancer screening including mammograms and pap smears;

- 80% of coverage for all physician prescribed equipment and supplies used in the management and treatment of diabetes not otherwise covered under Part D. Coverage must include persons with gestational, type I, or type II diabetes;

- coverage of cost sharing for all Part A eligible hospice care and respite care expenses; and

- coverage for cost sharing for Part A or Part B home health care services and medical supplies subject to the Medicare Part B deductible amount.

b. Riders The following benefit riders must be offered with the basic Medicare supplement plan:

- Coverage for all of the Medicare Part A inpatient hospital deductible amount

- One hundred percent of the Medicare Part B excess charges coverage for the difference between the actual Medicare Part B charges billed and the Medicare-approved Part B charge

- Coverage for all of the Medicare Part B annual deductible

- Preventive medical care coverage for the following preventative health services not covered by Medicare

  — An annual clinical preventive medical history and physical examination that may include screening tests, preventive services, and patient education to address preventive health care measures

  — Preventive screening tests or preventive services, the selection and frequency of which is determined to be medically appropriate by the attending physician (reimbursement shall be for the actual charges up to 100% of the Medicare-approved amount for each service, to a maximum of $120 annually under this benefit. This benefit does not pay for a procedure covered by Medicare.)

9. Extended Basic Medicare Supplement Plan

a. Coverage The extended basic supplement plan must have a level of coverage so that it will be certified as a qualified plan and will provide:

- coverage for all of the Part A inpatient hospital deductible and coinsurance amounts, and 100% of all Part A eligible hospitalization expenses not covered by Medicare;

- coverage for the daily co-payment amount of Medicare Part A eligible expenses for the calendar year incurred for skilled nursing facility care;

- coverage for the coinsurance amount or, where applicable, the co-payment amount of Medicare eligible expenses and the Medicare Part B deductible amount;

- 80% of the usual and customary hospital and medical expenses and supplies while outside the United States;

- 80% of prescription drug expenses not covered by Medicare. An outpatient prescription drug benefit must not be included in a Medicare supplement policy or certificate issued on or after January 1, 2006;

- coverage for the reasonable cost of the first three pints of blood or equivalent quantities of packed red blood cells; applies to Part A or Part B;

- 100% of the cost of immunizations not otherwise covered under Part D and routine screening procedures for cancer, including mammograms and pap smears;

- coverage for the following preventive health services not covered by Medicare:

  — An annual clinical preventive medical history and physical examination that may include screening tests, preventive services, and patient education to address preventive health care measures

  — Preventive screening tests or preventive services, the selection and frequency of which is determined to be medically appropriate by the attending physician

    - Reimbursement shall be for the actual charges up to 100% of the Medicare-approved amount for each service to a maximum of $120 annually under this benefit. This benefit shall not include payment for any procedure covered by Medicare;

- coverage of cost sharing for all Medicare Part A eligible hospice care and respite care expenses; and

- coverage for cost sharing for Medicare Part A or Part B home health care services and medical supplies.

10. Medicare Supplement Plan with High Deductible Coverage (Plan F)

a. Coverage The Medicare supplement plan will pay 100% coverage after payment of the annual high deductible. The annual deductible shall consist of out-of-pocket expenses, other than premiums, for covered services. The plan must have a level of coverage that will provide:

- 100% of Medicare Part A hospitalization coinsurance plus coverage for 365 days after Medicare benefits end;

- coverage for 100% of the Part A inpatient hospital deductible amount per benefit period;

- coverage for 100% of the daily coinsurance amount from day 21 through day 100 in a Medicare benefit period for post-hospital skilled nursing care eligible under Medicare Part A;

- coverage for 100% of cost sharing for all Part A eligible expenses and respite care;

- coverage for 100% of the reasonable cost of the first three pints of blood, or equivalent quantities of packed red blood cells; applies to Part A or Part B;

- coverage for 100% of the cost sharing otherwise applicable under Medicare Part B; does not apply if coverage is provided in this clause;

- coverage of 100% of the cost sharing for Part B preventive services and diagnostic procedures for cancer screening after the policyholder pays the Part B deductible;

- coverage of 100% of the hospital and medical expenses and supplies incurred during travel outside of the United States as a result of a medical emergency;

- coverage for 100% of Part A and Part B home health care services and medical supplies; and

- the deductible will be adjusted annually by the secretary of the United States Department of Health and Human Services to reflect the change in the Consumer Price Index for the 12-month period ending with August of the preceding year.

11. Medicare Supplement Plan with 50% Coverage (Plan K)

a. **Coverage** The Medicare supplement plan with 50% coverage must have a level of coverage that will provide:

- 100% of Medicare Part A hospitalization coinsurance plus coverage for 365 days after Medicare benefits end;

- coverage for 50% of the Part A inpatient hospital deductible amount per benefit period until the out-of-pocket limitation is met, which varies each year;

- coverage for 50% of the daily coinsurance amount from day 21 through day 100 in a Medicare benefit period for post-hospital skilled nursing care eligible under Part A until the out-of-pocket limitation is met;

- coverage for 50% of cost sharing for all Medicare Part A eligible expenses and respite care until the out-of-pocket limitation is met;

- coverage for 50% of the reasonable cost of the first three pints of blood, or equivalent quantities of packed red blood cells, until the out-of-pocket limitation is met; applies to Part A or Part B;

- except for coverage provided in this clause, coverage for 50% of the cost sharing otherwise applicable under Medicare Part B, after the policyholder pays the Medicare Part B deductible, until the out-of-pocket limitation is met;

- coverage of 100% of the cost sharing for Medicare Part B preventive services and diagnostic procedures for cancer screening after the policyholder pays the Medicare Part B deductible; and

- coverage of 100% of all cost sharing under Medicare Part A and Part B for the balance of the calendar year after the individual has reached the out-of-pocket limitation on annual expenditures. The out-of-pocket limitation under Medicare Part A and Part B is indexed each year by the appropriate inflation adjustment.

12. Medicare Supplement Plan with 75% Coverage (Plan L)

a. **Coverage** The Medicare supplement plan with 75% coverage must have a level of coverage that will provide:

- 100% of Medicare Part A hospitalization coinsurance plus coverage for 365 days after Medicare benefits end;

- coverage for 75% of the Part A inpatient hospital deductible amount per benefit period until the out-of-pocket limitation is met, which varies every year;

- coverage for 75% of the daily coinsurance amount from day 21 through day 100 in a Medicare benefit period for post-hospital skilled nursing care eligible under Part A until the out-of-pocket limitation is met;

- coverage for 75% of cost sharing for all Medicare Part A eligible expenses and respite care until the out-of-pocket limitation is met;

- coverage for 75% of the reasonable cost of the first three pints of blood, or equivalent quantities of packed red blood cells, until the out-of-pocket limitation is met; applies to Part A or Part B;

- except for coverage provided in this clause, coverage for 75% of the cost sharing otherwise applicable under Medicare Part B, after the policyholder pays the Medicare Part B deductible, until the out-of-pocket limitation is met;

- coverage of 100% of the cost sharing for Medicare Part B preventive services and diagnostic procedures for cancer screening after the policyholder pays the Medicare Part B deductible; and

- coverage of 100% of all cost sharing under Medicare Part A and Part B for the balance of the calendar year after the individual has reached the out-of-pocket limitation on annual expenditures. The out-of-pocket limitation under Medicare Part A and Part B is indexed each year by the appropriate inflation adjustment.

13. Medicare Supplement Plan with 50% Part A Deductible Coverage (Plan M)

a. **Coverage** The Medicare supplement plan with 50% Medicare Part A deductible coverage must have a level of coverage that will provide:

- 100% of Medicare Part A hospitalization coinsurance plus coverage for 365 days after Medicare benefits end;

- coverage for 50% of the Part A inpatient hospital deductible amount per benefit period;

- coverage for the daily coinsurance amount from day 21 through day 100 in a Medicare benefit period for post-hospital skilled nursing care eligible under Part A;

- coverage for cost sharing for all Medicare Part A eligible hospice and respite care expenses;

- coverage for the reasonable cost of the first three pints of blood, or equivalent quantities of packed red blood cells; applies to Part A or Part B;

- coverage for 100% of the cost sharing otherwise applicable under Medicare Part B, after the policyholder pays the Medicare Part B deductible;

- coverage of 100% of the cost sharing for Medicare Part B preventive services and diagnostic procedures for cancer screening after the policyholder pays the Medicare Part B deductible;

- coverage of 80% of the hospital and medical expenses and supplies incurred during travel outside of the United States as a result of a medical emergency; and

- coverage for 100% of the Medicare Part A or Part B home health care services and medical supplies after the policyholder pays the Medicare Part B deductible.

14. Medicare Supplement Plan with $20 and $50 Co-payment Medicare Part B Coverage (Plan N)

a. **Coverage** The Medicare supplement plan with $20 and $50 co-payment Medicare Part B coverage must have a level of coverage that will provide:

- 100% of Medicare Part A hospitalization coinsurance plus coverage for 365 days after Medicare benefits end;

- coverage for the Part A inpatient hospital deductible amount per benefit period;

- coverage for the daily coinsurance amount from day 21 through day 100 in a Medicare benefit period for post-hospital skilled nursing care eligible under Part A;

- coverage for the cost sharing for all Medicare Part A eligible hospice and respite care expenses;

- coverage for the reasonable cost of the first three pints of blood, or equivalent quantities of packed red blood cells; applies to Part A or Part B;

- coverage for 100% of the cost sharing applicable under Medicare Part B except for the lesser of $20 or the Part B coinsurance or co-payment for each covered office visit; and the lesser of $50 or the Part B coinsurance or co-payment for each covered emergency room visit. The co-payment will be waived if the insured is admitted to any hospital and the emergency visit is subsequently covered as a Medicare Part A expense;

- coverage of 100% of the cost sharing for Medicare Part B preventive services and diagnostic procedures for cancer screening after the policyholder pays the Medicare Part B deductible;

- coverage of 80% of the hospital and medical expenses and supplies incurred during travel outside of the United States as a result of a medical emergency; and

- coverage for Medicare Part A or Part B home health care services and medical supplies after the policyholder pays the Medicare Part B deductible.

D. LONG-TERM CARE (LTC) [60K.365; 62A.46-.56; 62S]
Long-term care is care needed for an extended period of time to deal with the prolonged effects of illness, injury or old age. LTC insurance is used to reimburse expenses such as nursing home care, assisted living facility care, and home care.

1. **Policy requirements** Only qualified insurers can offer, issue, or deliver individual and group long-term care policies, and all policies must satisfy the statute requirements. A long-term care policy must cover prescribed long-term care in nursing facilities or the prescribed long-term home care services provided by a home health agency. The policy may also cover both types of services.

   a. **Coverage** Coverage under a long-term care policy, other than one that covers only nursing facility services, must include: a minimum lifetime benefit limit of at least $25,000 for services. A policy that covers only nursing facility services must include a minimum lifetime benefit limit of at least one year. A separate lifetime maximum will not apply to policies that cover both nursing facility and home health care. Prior hospitalization is not required under a long-term care policy.

   b. **Preexisting conditions** The policy must cover preexisting conditions during the first six months of coverage if the insured was not diagnosed or treated for the particular condition during the 90 days immediately preceding the effective date of coverage. Coverage may include a waiting period of up to 180 days, but there can be no more than one waiting period per benefit period. A policy may not exclude coverage for mental or nervous disorders such as Alzheimer's and related dementias. Policies cannot require the insured to be homebound or confined to their house in order to receive home care services.

c. **Free-look provision** Policyholders who are not satisfied with the policy for any reason may return it within 30 days of its delivery and receive a full refund, less any benefits paid.

d. **Cancellation provision** The policy must include a provision that the plan will not be cancelled or nonrenewed for any reason other than non payment of premium. The insured must designate at least one person, in addition to the insured, who will receive the policy cancellation notice for nonpayment of premium. The insured has the right to designate up to three people, in addition to the insured, who will receive the notice of cancellation. Each time an individual policy is renewed or continued, the insurer shall notify the insured of the right to change the written designation. Prior to cancelling a policy for nonpayment of premium, the insurer must provide the insured and those designated at least 30 days notice before the effective date of cancellation.

e. **Coordination of benefits** There is no coordination of benefits between a long-term care policy and an accident and health policy, disability policy, or accident only policy.

2. **Home care services** Policies for home care services only may be sold provided they meet statutory requirements. Disclosures and representations regarding these policies must be adjusted accordingly to remove references to coverage for nursing home care.

a. **Prohibited limitations** A long-term care policy or certificate that provides benefits for home health care or community care services may not limit or exclude benefits by doing any of the following:

1.) Requiring that the insured would need care in a skilled nursing facility if home health care services were not provided

2.) Requiring that the insured first or simultaneously receive nursing or therapeutic services in a home, community, or institutional setting before home health care services are covered

3.) Limiting eligible services to those provided only by a registered nurse or licensed practical nurse

4.) Requiring that a nurse or therapist provide services that are covered by the policy instead of having those services provided by a home health aide or other licensed or certified home care worker who is acting within the scope of their licensure or certification

5.) Excluding coverage for personal care services provided by a home health aide

6.) Requiring that the provision of home health care services be at a level of certification or licensure greater than what is required by the eligible service

7.) Requiring that the insured have an acute condition before home health care services get covered

8.) Limiting benefits to only those services provided by Medicare-certified agencies or providers

9.) Excluding coverage for adult day care services

10.) Excluding coverage based upon location or type of residence in which the home health care services would be provided

3. **Disclosures and representations** A policy not intended to be a qualified long-term care insurance policy must include a disclosure statement within the policy and a coverage outline of that fact. The disclosure should be prominently displayed and read as follows: "This long-term care insurance policy (certificate) is not intended to be a qualified long-term care insurance contract as defined under section 7702 (B)(b) of the Internal Revenue Code of 1986. You should consult with your attorney, accountant, or tax advisor regarding the tax implications of purchasing long-term care insurance."

   a. **Government endorsements** Policies and promotional literature may not display a seal or emblem implying that the policy is approved, endorsed, or certified by the local, state, or federal government.

   b. **Cancellation notice** Individual long-term care policies must have a notice prominently printed on the first page stating that the policyholder may return the policy within 30 days of its delivery and receive a full refund if the policyholder is not satisfied for any reason.

   c. **Disclosures** At the time of application for an individual or group long-term care policy a statement containing the following disclosures must be delivered to the applicant.

      1.) A description of the benefits and coverage provided by the policy and the differences between the long-term care policy, a Medicare supplement policy and the benefits to which an individual is entitled under parts A and B of Medicare

      2.) A statement of the exceptions and limitations in the policy including the following language, as applicable, in bold print: "**THIS POLICY DOES NOT COVER ALL NURSING CARE FACILITIES OR NURSING HOME, HOME CARE, OR ADULT DAY CARE EXPENSES AND DOES NOT COVER RESIDENTIAL CARE. READ YOUR POLICY CAREFULLY TO DETERMINE WHICH FACILITIES AND EXPENSES ARE COVERED BY YOUR POLICY.**"

3.) A statement of the renewal provisions including the insurer's right to change premiums

4.) A statement that the outline of coverage is a summary of the policy issued or for which was applied, and that the policy should be consulted to determine governing contractual provisions

5.) A statement of the out-of-pocket expenses, including deductibles and co-payments for which the insured is responsible, and an explanation of the specific out-of-pocket expenses that may be accumulated toward any out-of-pocket maximum

6.) The following language, in bold print: "**YOUR PREMIUMS CAN BE INCREASED IN THE FUTURE. THE RATE SCHEDULE THAT LISTS YOUR PREMIUM NOW CAN CHANGE.**"

7.) A statement explaining the waiting period for nursing care services and home care services

8.) At the time of application, a signed and completed copy of the insurance application is left with the applicant

9.) The insurer may review an insured's plan of care at reasonable intervals, but not more frequently than once every 30 days.

4. Prohibited practices The solicitation or sale of long-term care policies is subject to the requirements and penalties that apply to the sale of Medicare supplement insurance policies found in statutes 62A.31-.44. It is an act of misconduct for an agent or company to make misstatements concerning eligibility or coverage under the medical assistance program, or about how long-term care costs will or will not be financed if a person does not have long-term care insurance. An agent or company providing information on the medical assistance program shall also provide information about how to contact the county human services department or the state Department of Human Services.

5. Qualified long-term care insurance [62S] A tax-qualified, long-term care policy offers certain federal income tax advantages to the purchaser. The benefits received are generally not considered taxable income, and some or all of the premiums can be deducted as medical expenses in accordance with tax laws.

a. Requirements Coverage must refer to at least five activities of daily living. Assessments of activities of daily living and cognitive impairment must be performed by a licensed or certified professional, such as a physician, nurse, or social worker. The policy shall not provide a cash surrender value, or other money that can be paid or used as collateral for a loan, or that can be borrowed. In the event of the insured's death or a complete surrender or cancellation of the policy, the aggregate premium paid may be refunded.

1.) Nonforfeiture requirement An insurer shall offer a nonforfeiture provision available if the insured defaults on any premium payments. The provision must provide at least one of the following:

- Reduced paid-up insurance
- Extended term insurance
- Shortened benefit period

2.) Long-term care insurance policies and certificates must include a provision that provides for reinstatement of coverage, in the event of lapse, if the insurer is provided proof of cognitive impairment or the loss of functional capacity. This option must be available to the insured if requested within five months after termination and must allow for the collection of past due premium, where appropriate.

3.) The standard of proof of cognitive impairment or loss of functional capacity shall not be more stringent than the benefit eligibility criteria on cognitive impairment or the loss of functional capacity, if any, contained in the policy and certificate.

b. Prohibitions A long-term care insurance policy may not:

- be cancelled, nonrenewed, or terminated on the grounds of the insured's or certificate holder's age or the deterioration of their mental or physical health;
- contain a provision establishing a new waiting period if existing coverage is converted to or replaced by a new form within the same company. The exception is if the insured or group policyholder voluntarily selects an increase in benefits; or
- provide coverage for skilled nursing care only, or provide significantly more coverage for skilled care in a facility than coverage for lower levels of care in the same facility.

c. Preexisting conditions *Preexisting condition* means a condition for which medical advice or treatment was recommended by, or received from, a health care services provider within six months prior to the insured's effective date of coverage.

1.) An individual long-term care insurance policy or certificate may not exclude coverage for a loss or confinement that is the result of a preexisting condition more than six months following the insured's effective date of coverage.

2.) The definition of preexisting condition does not prohibit an insurer from using an application form designed to obtain the complete health history of an applicant. On the basis of the answers on the application, the insurer may underwrite the applicant according to the insurer's established underwriting standards. Unless otherwise provided in the policy or certificate, a preexisting condition, regardless of whether it is disclosed on the application, need not be covered until the waiting period of six months expires. A long-term care insurance policy or certificate may not exclude or use waivers of any kind to exclude, limit, or reduce coverage or benefits for specifically named or described preexisting diseases or physical conditions beyond the six month waiting period.

3.) The Commissioner may extend the six-month limitation periods for specific age groups in specific policy forms if the Commissioner finds that the extension is in the best interest of the public.

d. **Right to return** Policyholders who are not satisfied with the policy for any reason may return it within 30 days of its delivery and receive a full refund. The *free-look* provision notice must be prominently printed or attached to the first page of the policy. If an application is denied, the applicant will receive a refund of any submitted premium and fees within 30 days of the denial.

e. **Outline of coverage** An outline of coverage must be delivered to a prospective applicant at the time of initial solicitation. In the case of agent solicitations, an agent must deliver the outline of coverage before the presentation of an application or enrollment form. In the case of direct response solicitations, the outline of coverage must be presented with an application or enrollment form. The outline must contain the following information:

1.) The policy must be identified as an individual or group policy.

2.) The outline of coverage provides a very brief description of the important features of the policy. The applicant should read the policy or certificate carefully for the governing contractual provisions and rights and obligations of both parties.

3.) The plan is designed to be a qualified long-term care insurance contract as defined by the Internal Revenue Code.

4.) Whether or not the policy is guaranteed renewable or noncancelable and the meaning of each.

5.) Whether or not the insurer has a right to change the premium, and if so, a clear and concise description of each circumstance under which the premium may change.

6.) Provide a brief description of the right to return the policy, also known as the *free-look* provision.

7.) The policy is not Medicare supplement coverage. If eligible for Medicare, the applicant should review the *Medicare Supplement Buyer's Guide*. Neither the insurer nor its agents represent Medicare, the federal government or any state government.

8.) The policy provides coverage for long-term care expenses subject to the policy limitations, waiting periods, and coinsurance requirements.

9.) Activities of daily living and cognitive impairment shall be used to measure an insured's need for long-term care and must be defined and described as part of the outline of coverage. Benefits provided by the policy include:

- covered services, related deductibles, waiting period, elimination periods, and benefit maximums;
- institutional benefits, by skill level;
- noninstitutional benefits, by skill level; and
- eligibility for payment of benefits.

10.) The outline shall advise that the policy many not cover all expenses associated with the insured's long-term care needs. The following limitations and exclusions should be described:

- Preexisting conditions
- Noneligible facilities or providers
- Noneligible levels of care
- Exclusions or exceptions
- Limitations

11.) Because the costs of long-term care services will likely increase, the outline should list any provisions or options that allow the insured to purchase additional benefits and how they will be increased.

12.) The policy provides coverage for insureds that are clinically diagnosed with Alzheimer's disease or related degenerative and dementing illnesses. The outline should describe any provisions that provide preconditions to the availability of policy benefits.

13.) Identify the total annual premium for the policy and the premium amount for each benefit option.

14.) Indicate if medical underwriting is used and describe other important features.

15.) The applicant is advised to contact the insurer with specific questions about the policy or certificate, and the Minnesota Department of Commerce or Senior Linkage Line with general questions regarding long-term care insurance.

f.   Claim denial If a claim is denied, the policy issuer shall provide a written explanation of the reasons for denial and provide all information related to the denial within 60 days of any written request by the policyholder, certificate holder, or their representative.

g.   Incontestability period It is possible for an insurer to withdraw the policy or deny a claim if the insured has misrepresented information on the original application. The determining factors are the length of time the policy has been in place, and the relevance of the information as it relates to the claim. (If an insurer has paid benefits under the long-term care insurance policy or certificate, the benefit payments may not be recovered by the insurer in the event that the policy or certificate is rescinded.)

1.) For a policy or certificate that has been in force for less than six months, an insurer may rescind the policy or certificate, or deny an otherwise valid claim if the insured made a material (relevant) misrepresentation on their application.

2.) For a policy or certificate that has been in force for at least six months, but less than two years, an insurer may rescind the policy or certificate, or deny an otherwise valid claim if the insured made a material misrepresentation on their application and it pertains to the condition for which benefits are sought.

3.) After a policy or certificate has been in force for two years, it is not contestable upon the grounds of misrepresentation alone. The policy or certificate may be contested only if the insured knowingly and intentionally misrepresented relevant facts relating to the insured's health.

h. Guaranteed renewable A qualified long-term care insurance policy must be guaranteed renewable. An individual policy must be guaranteed renewable or noncancelable. The term "level premium" may only be used when the insurer does not have the right to change the premium.

i. Inflation protection Insurers must offer a policy with an inflation protection feature with one of the following options:

- Benefit increases that compound annually at a minimum of 5%
- A guarantee that the insured has the right to periodically increase benefit levels without providing evidence of insurability or health status
- Coverage for a specified percentage of actual or reasonable charges without a maximum specified indemnity amount or limit

1.) Benefit increases under a policy that contains inflation protection must continue without regard to an insured's age, claim status or claim history, or the length of time the person has been insured under the policy.

2.) Inflation protection must be included in a long-term care insurance policy unless the buyer formally rejects it. The signed rejection may be either in the application or on a separate form. The rejection shall be considered a part of the application.

j. Authorized limitations and exclusions Typically, a long-term care policy issued or delivered in Minnesota may not limit or exclude coverage by type of illness, treatment, or medical condition. There are, however, exceptions to that law. The following illnesses, treatments, or medical conditions **can be limited or excluded from coverage:**

- Preexisting conditions or diseases

■ Mental or nervous disorders; however, the exclusion or limitation of benefits on the basis of Alzheimer's disease is prohibited

■ Alcoholism and drug addiction

■ Illness, treatment, or medical condition arising out of war or an act of war; participation in a felony; service in the armed forces; suicide, attempted suicide, or an intentionally self-inflicted injury; or non-fare-paying aviation

■ Treatment provided in a government facility unless otherwise required by law

■ Benefits available under Medicare or another government program with the exception of Medicaid, state or federal workers' compensation, employer's liability or occupational disease law, or motor vehicle no-fault law

■ Services provided by a member of the covered person's immediate family, and services for which no charge is normally made in the absence of insurance

■ Benefits covered under another long-term care insurance or health insurance policy

■ In the case of a qualified long-term care insurance contract, expenses that are reimbursable through Social Security

k. Continuation or conversion Group long-term care insurance shall provide covered individuals with a basis for continuation or conversion of coverage if continuously covered for at least six months prior to termination from the group plan.

1.) Continuation The continuation of coverage provision allows for the insured to maintain coverage under the existing group policy when the coverage would otherwise terminate. The insured is required to continue the timely payment of premium. Continuation benefits will be substantially equivalent to the benefits of the existing group policy.

2.) Conversion A converted long-term care policy must provide benefits identical to, substantially equivalent to, or in excess of those provided under the original group policy. Written application for the converted policy must be made, and the first premium paid, no later than 31 days after termination of coverage under the group policy. The converted policy must be effective on the day following the terminated coverage and is renewable annually.

a.) If an individual is covered by another long-term care policy, the converted policy may contain a provision in which the benefits payable will be reduced if the total benefit amount from the two policies would result in payment of more than the actual incurred expenses.

b.) The premium for the converted policy is calculated on the basis of the insured's age at inception of coverage under the group policy from which conversion is made.

l. Replacement If a group long-term care policy is replaced by another group policy issued to the same policyholder, the new insurer shall offer coverage to all persons covered under the previous group policy. Coverage provided or offered, and premiums charged under the new group policy, shall not result in any exclusion for preexisting conditions that would have been covered under the old group policy. Coverage and premiums can not vary or depend on the individual's health or disability status, claim experience, or use of long-term care services.

1.) The premiums charged for a replacement policy shall not increase due to the length of time the insured has been covered under the replaced policy, nor because of the increasing age of the insured beyond age 65.

2.) The purchase of additional coverage is not considered a premium rate increase but will be added to the initial annual premium.

3.) A reduction in benefits is not considered a premium change, but the initial annual premium will be based on the reduced benefits.

m. Disclosure provisions Long-term care policies have certain policy requirements, limitations, or insurer rights that must be clearly stated within the policy, or at times on the first page of the policy.

1.) Coverage under an individual long-term care policy is guaranteed renewable or noncancelable. This renewability provision must be clearly stated on the first page of the policy. If the insurer has the right to change the premium, the policy or certificate shall include a statement to that effect.

2.) Any riders or endorsements that are added to an individual long-term care policy after the policy is issued, reinstated, or renewed, and which increase, reduce, or eliminate benefits or coverage, must be agreed to in writing by the insured. Written agreement is not required if the increased benefits or coverage are required by law. The additional premium associated with riders or endorsements must be specified in the policy, rider, or endorsement.

3.) If a long-term care insurance policy provides benefits based on standards described as *usual and customary, reasonable and customary,* or similar words the outline of coverage must include a definition and explanation of those terms.

4.) If a long-term care policy or certificate contains any limitations with respect to preexisting conditions, the limitations must appear as a separate paragraph of the policy or certificate and must be labeled as *preexisting condition limitations.*

5.) A long-term care insurance policy or certificate that contains any limitations or conditions for eligibility must provide a description of the limitations or conditions, including any required number of days of confinement, in a separate paragraph of the policy or certificate. The paragraph should be labeled the *limitations or conditions on eligibility for benefits.*

6.) Life insurance policies that provide an accelerated benefit for long-term care require a disclosure statement at the time of policy or rider application and at the same time the accelerated benefit payment request is submitted. The statement must advise that the accelerated benefits received may be taxable, and that assistance should be sought from a personal tax advisor. The disclosure statement must be prominently displayed on the first page of the policy or rider, as well as on any other related documents. This requirement does not apply to qualified long-term care insurance contracts.

7.) Activities of daily living and cognitive impairment must be used to measure an insured's need for long-term care and must be described in the policy or certificate in a separate paragraph labeled *Eligibility for the Payment of Benefits*. Any additional benefit triggers must also be explained in this section. If these triggers differ for different benefits, an explanation of the trigger must accompany each benefit description. If the policy requires an attending physician or other specified person to certify a certain level of functional dependency for the insured to be eligible for benefits, this too must be specified.

8.) A qualified long-term care insurance policy must include a disclosure statement that the policy is intended to be a qualified long-term care insurance policy under section 7702B(b) of the Internal Revenue Code of 1986, as amended.

n. Marketing Standards Marketing and advertising of long-term care policies is closely regulated by the Commissioner to ensure that producers and insurers follow specific guidelines when selling policies, and to ensure the public is aware and informed of the coverage, benefits, and limitations prior to purchasing a policy.

1.) An insurer or other entity marketing long-term care insurance coverage in Minnesota, directly or through its producers, shall:
- establish marketing procedures and agent training requirements to ensure that any marketing activities, including policy comparisons by its agents or other producers, are fair and accurate;
- establish marketing procedures to assure excessive insurance is not sold or issued;
- display prominently on the first page of the outline of coverage and policy, the following: "Notice to buyer: This policy may not cover all of the costs associated with long-term care incurred by the buyer during the period of coverage. The buyer is advised to review carefully all policy limitations.";
- provide copies of the disclosure forms to the applicant per the required statute;
- determine whether a prospective applicant or enrollee already has long-term care insurance and the types and amounts of the insurance;
- establish procedures for verifying compliance with the statute, which can be audited;

- if applicable, provide written notice to the prospective policyholder and certificate holder, at the time of solicitation, that the Senior LinkAge Line, a senior insurance counseling program approved by the Commissioner, is available. Also provide the name, address, and telephone number of the program;

- use the terms *noncancelable* or *level premium* only when the policy or certificate is guaranteed renewable or if premiums will not change; and

- provide an explanation of contingent benefit upon lapse provided for in nonforfeiture requirements.

2.) Prohibitions The following acts and practices are prohibited:

- Knowingly inducing a person to lapse, forfeit, surrender, terminate, or convert any insurance policy by making misleading representations or incomplete or fraudulent comparisons of other insurance policies or insurers

- Using marketing to induce the purchase of insurance through coercion, threats or undue pressure

- Failing to disclose that a purpose of the marketing is the solicitation of insurance and that an insurance agent or insurance company will contact the prospect

- Misrepresenting a material fact when selling or offering to sell a policy

3.) Association disclosure requirements The primary responsibility of an association, when endorsing or selling long-term care insurance, is to educate its members concerning long-term care issues in general so that its members can make informed decisions. Associations must provide objective information regarding long-term care insurance policies or certificates endorsed or sold by the associations to ensure that members receive a balanced and complete explanation of policy features and benefits. Also, the association must disclose the specific nature and amount of the compensation arrangements.

o. Suitability in solicitation One of the most important jobs of a producer is to determine the suitability of the insurance product being proposed to the applicant. Because the producer is in a position to know much more about the product than the consumer, the insurance Commissioner places great emphasis on the producer's duty to help the consumer make an informed decision.

1.) Standards Every insurer or entity marketing long-term care insurance shall:

- develop and use suitability standards to determine whether the purchase or replacement of long-term care insurance is appropriate for the needs of the applicant;

- train its agents in the use of its suitability standards; and

- maintain a copy of its suitability standards and make them available for inspection upon request by the Commissioner.

2.) Procedures To determine whether the applicant meets the standards developed by the insurer or entity marketing long-term care insurance, the agent and insurer or entity shall develop procedures that take into consideration the ability to pay for the proposed coverage, the applicant's goals or needs with respect to long-term care, and a comparison of any existing insurance owned by the applicant.

3.) Forms Prior to application, the insurer or agent should provide the applicant with two forms: The *Long-Term Care Insurance Personal Worksheet* and the disclosure form entitled *Things You Should Know Before You Buy Long-Term Care Insurance*. The worksheet must be completed and returned prior to considering the applicant for coverage. However, the worksheet does not need to be returned for sales of employer group long-term care insurance.

p. Shopper's Guide A long-term care insurance shopper's guide must be provided to all prospective applicants. In the case of agent solicitations, an agent must deliver the shopper's guide before presenting the application or enrollment form. In the case of direct response solicitations, the shopper's guide must be presented with the application or enrollment form. This requirement does not apply to life insurance policies or riders containing accelerated long-term care benefits.

q. Penalties An insurer or agent who violates a Minnesota statute relating to the regulation or marketing of long-term care insurance can be fined up to three times the amount of any commissions paid for each policy involved in the violation to a maximum of $10,000.

6. Long-term care training requirements Legislation requires that anyone who intends to solicit, sell, or negotiate long-term care insurance policies in Minnesota be licensed as an insurance producer for accident and health insurance and life insurance if the producer plans to sell long-term care riders. In addition, the individual must complete an initial training course and subsequent ongoing training every two years.

a. Training course The initial training course must be at least eight hours; ongoing training courses must be at least four hours, and must be taken every two years. Courses must be approved by the Commissioner, and may be approved for continuing education. Courses must consist of topics related to long-term care insurance, long-term care services, and qualified state long-term care insurance partnership programs, including, but not limited to:

- state and federal regulations and requirements;
- the relationship between qualified state long-term care insurance partnership programs and other public and private coverage of long-term care services, including Medicaid/Minnesota medical assistance;
- available long-term care services and providers;
- changes or improvements in long-term care services or providers;
- alternatives to the purchase of private long-term care insurance;

■ the effect of inflation on benefits and the importance of inflation protection; and

■ consumer suitability standards and guidelines.

b. **Verification of completion** Insurers must verify that a producer has completed the required training before a producer is permitted to sell, solicit, or negotiate the insurer's long-term care insurance products. Insurers shall maintain records verifying that the producer has received the training and provide verification to the Commissioner upon request.

c. **Training in other states** Satisfying these initial training requirements in any state satisfies the initial training requirements of Minnesota.

d. **Nonresident producers** Nonresident producers selling partnership policies are expected to demonstrate knowledge about unique aspects of the Minnesota medical assistance system. An insurer offering partnership products in Minnesota shall maintain records verifying that its nonresident producers have obtained the required training and provide verification to the Commissioner upon request.

E. **HEALTH MAINTENANCE ORGANIZATIONS (HMOs) [62D]** Health maintenance organizations combine the financing and delivery of health care. Subscribers pay a flat monthly fee in exchange for access to a select network of health care providers. In turn, the health care providers typically receive a fixed payment per subscriber that does not vary with the amount of care provided. Nonprofit corporations or local governmental units may also, upon obtaining a certificate of authority from the Commissioner of health, operate as a health maintenance organization or Health Service organization. Nonprofit regulation is covered in the following [62C].

1. **Health maintenance contract** HMOs agree to provide comprehensive health maintenance services to enrollees as set forth in the health maintenance contract.

2. **Comprehensive health maintenance services** These plans offer health services required to maintain good health and prevent disease. These services include, but are not limited to, emergency care, emergency ground ambulance transportation, inpatient hospital and physician care, outpatient health services, and preventive health services.

3. **Evidence of coverage** A health maintenance organization will issue evidence of coverage or contract to its Minnesota enrollees by the effective date, or for groups, within 15 days of the effective date. The evidence of coverage or contract and any amendments must be filed with the Commissioner of health. Contracts and evidences of coverage may not contain provisions or statements that are unjust, unfair, misleading, or deceptive.

a. **Required provisions** The contracts and evidences of coverage shall contain a clear, concise, and complete statement of the following:
■ The health care services and the insurance or other benefits to which the enrollee is entitled

- Any exclusions or limitations on the services and benefits, including any deductible or co-payment feature, and requirements for referrals, prior authorizations, and second opinions

- How the enrollee can obtain information about the availability of services, including emergency and out of area services

- The total amount of applicable payment and co-payment for health care services and the applicable portion the enrollee is obligated to pay with respect to individual contracts; included should be an indication whether the plan is contributory or noncontributory (employee or employer paid) with respect to group certificates

- A description of the health maintenance organization's method for resolving enrollee complaints and a statement identifying the Commissioner as an external source with whom complaints may be registered

b. Enrollees' rights The cover page of the evidence of coverage and contract will include important enrollee information and a clear and complete statement of the enrollees' rights. The enrollee information will include the following.

- Procedures the enrollee must follow to obtain coverage from the HMO will be included.

- Only services from providers that are part of the health maintenance organization will be covered, and certain services are covered only upon referral.

- Emergency services from providers not affiliated with the HMO are covered 24/7. Benefits and procedures associated with emergency care are explained in the contract.

- Certain services of medical supplies are not covered. The exclusions are detailed in the contract.

- The enrollee may convert to an individual health maintenance organization contract or continue coverage under certain circumstances. Those rights are fully explained in the contract.

- The contract describes all reasons for cancellation of coverage, which can be initiated by the enrollee or the HMO.

- For plans providing dependent coverage, a newborn is covered from birth but only if services are provided by the HMO providers or authorized by the HMO. Certain services are covered only upon referral. The enrollee should notify the health maintenance organization of the birth and the need for coverage. At that time, any required additional premium is due.

- Enrollment in the health maintenance organization does not guarantee a particular prescription drug or particular piece of medical equipment will be available.

c. Grace period Beginning with the second premium payment, a grace period of 31 days is granted for payment of each premium due for an individual health maintenance contract. The contract will remain in force during the grace period.

d. Free-look period A person may cancel an individual health maintenance contract within 10 days of receipt, and receive a refund of premium paid, if after examining the contract the individual is not satisfied for any reason. The individual is responsible for repaying the HMO for any services rendered or claims paid during the 10 days.

e. **Notice of changes** Individual and group contract holders will be given 30 days advance written notice of any change in subscriber fees or benefits.

4. **Information to enrollees** Once enrolled, a subscriber is provided information from the health maintenance organization regarding participating providers, Medicare information, and membership cards. Any marketing materials used with potential enrollees will include a statement of enrollee information and rights.

   a. **Medicare information** Health maintenance organizations issuing contracts to people covered by Medicare must provide the applicant, at the time of application, with an outline containing the following information:

   - A description of the principal benefits and coverage provided in the contract, including a clear description of nursing home and home care benefits covered by the health maintenance organization

   - A statement of the exceptions, reductions, and limitations contained in the contract

   - The following language: "This contract does not cover all skilled nursing home care or home care services and does not cover custodial or residential nursing care. Read your contract carefully to determine which nursing home facilities and home care services are covered by your contract, and what procedures you must follow to receive these benefits."

   - A statement of the renewal provisions including the health maintenance organization's right to change fees, if applicable

   - A statement that the outline of coverage is a summary of the contract issued or applied for and that the contract should be read to determine governing contractual provisions

   - A statement explaining that the enrollee's Medicare coverage is altered by enrollment with the health maintenance organization, if applicable

   b. **Participating providers** An HMO will provide enrollees with a list of names and locations of participating providers to whom enrollees have direct access without needing a referral. The list of providers will include the publication date and a statement directing the enrollee to contact the provider to confirm coverage in the health maintenance organization. Within the health maintenance organization's service area, the maximum travel distance or time to seek primary care shall be the lesser of 30 miles or 30 minutes to the nearest provider. Within a service area, the maximum travel distance or time shall be the lesser of 60 miles or 60 minutes to the nearest provider of specialty physician services, ancillary services, specialized hospital services, and all other health services not considered primary care.

   c. **Requests for information** Information about how to obtain referrals, prior authorization, or a second opinion shall be given to the enrollee or an enrollee's representative in person or by telephone within one business day following receipt of the request.

d. **Marketing requirements** Written marketing materials directed toward potential enrollees and that include a detailed description of HMO benefits must include a statement of enrollee information and rights. Prior to any oral marketing presentation, the agent must inform potential enrollees that any complaints concerning the material should be directed to the health maintenance organization, the Commissioner of health, or if applicable, the employer.

   1.) Detailed marketing materials, excluding billboards and name identification advertisements, must disclose all exclusions and limitations of services including but not limited to:
   - health care services not provided;
   - health care services requiring co-payments or deductibles paid by enrollees;
   - the fact that access to health care services does not guarantee access to a particular provider type; and
   - health care services that require a physician's referral.

   2.) Marketing materials may not imply that all health care needs will be covered. All materials must alert consumers to possible uncovered expenses and advise consumers to read the contract carefully. In addition, consumers must be provided with contact information for questions regarding access to provider types.

   3.) Health maintenance organizations may not knowingly permit the use of advertising or solicitation that is untrue, misleading, or deceptive.

5. **Cost sharing** A health maintenance contract may contain enrollee cost-sharing provisions, such as co-payments, deductibles, and out-of-pocket maximums. Co-payment and deductible provisions in a group contract can not discriminate on the basis of age, sex, race, disability, economic status, or length of enrollment in the health plan. During an open enrollment period in which there are no underwriting restrictions, co-payment and deductible provisions must not discriminate on the basis of preexisting health status. Effective January 1, 2014, all cost sharing mechanisms will be consistent with the Affordable Care Act Section 62A.011.

   a. **Co-payments** A health maintenance contract may impose a flat fee co-payment on office visits and outpatient prescription drugs. Co-payments may not be charged for preventive health care services.

   b. **Deductibles** A health maintenance contract may impose deductibles on a per person/per year and a per family/per year basis. Deductibles may not be imposed on preventive health care services.

   c. **Annual out-of-pocket maximums** A health maintenance contract may include an annual out-of-pocket maximum on a per person and per family basis.

   d. **Public programs** Cost sharing does not apply to the prepaid medical assistance program, MinnesotaCare program, prepaid general assistance program, federal Medicare program, or health plans provided through any of those programs.

6. **Open enrollment provisions** Health plans provide an annual open enroll-ment period that must extend at least 14 days. During this time, HMOs accept for coverage all applying eligible individuals in a manner that does not discriminate on the basis of age, sex, race, health, or economic status. A health plan may apply to the Commissioner of health for a waiver of the requirements, or for authorization to impose underwriting restrictions during open enrollment to preserve its financial stability, to prevent excessive adverse selection by prospective enrollees, or to avoid unreasonably high or unmarketable charges for enrollee coverage. The Commissioner of health will approve or deny the waiver request within 30 days of receipt depending on whether or not the health plan shows good cause.

7. **Divorce** A health maintenance contract that provides coverage for the enrollee's spouse may not contain a provision for termination of coverage for the spouse solely as a result of divorce.

   a. **Continuation** Every health maintenance contract shall contain a provision that permits continuation of coverage for the enrollee's former spouse and children upon furnishing a divorce decree. The coverage shall be continued until the earlier of the following dates:

      ■ The date the enrollee's former spouse becomes covered under any other group plan or Medicare

      ■ The date coverage would otherwise terminate under the health maintenance contract

      1.) If coverage is provided under a group policy, the enrollee will pay any required premium on a monthly basis to the group contract holder who will remit the payment to the health maintenance organization. The con-tract must require the group contract holder to provide the enrollee with written verification of the coverage cost promptly at the time of eligibility and at any time during the continuation period.

      2.) At no time shall the premium charged exceed 102% of the plan cost. Upon request by the enrollee's former spouse or dependent child, a health maintenance organization must provide the necessary instructions to enable the spouse or dependent to elect continuation of coverage.

   b. **Conversion** Every health maintenance contract shall contain a provision allowing the enrollee's former spouse and dependent children, without providing evidence of insurability, to obtain conversion coverage from the health mainte-nance organization. The conversion coverage will be effective at the expiration of any continuation of coverage and will provide at least the minimum benefits of a qualified plan at premiums based on her original age of coverage. The appli-cation and premium payment must be made to the health maintenance organiza-tion within 30 days following notice of the expiration of the continued coverage. The individual health maintenance contract is renewable at the option of the former spouse provided that person is not covered under another qualified plan.

      1.) Effective January 1, 2014, an individual policy or contract issued as a conversion policy prior to January 1, 2014, will be renewable at the option of the covered person as long as the covered person is not covered under another qualified plan. Any revisions in the table of rate for the individual policy will apply to the insured's original age at entry and apply equally to all similar conversion policies."

8. **Current spouse and children** Minnesota law authorizes lawful civil marriage between two persons, including between persons of the same sex. As a result, after August 1, 2013, any policy issued in Minnesota that provides dependent coverage for spouses must make that coverage available on the same terms and conditions regardless of the sex of the spouse. A health maintenance contract that provides coverage to the enrollee's spouse and dependent children shall allow the spouse and dependent children to elect to continue coverage when the enrollee becomes enrolled for benefits under Medicare, and allow the dependent children to continue coverage when they cease to be dependent children under the plan's generally applicable requirement. A dependent child under ACA (Affordable Care Act) may extend to age 26, if certain qualifications are met.

   a. The coverage may be continued until the earlier of the following dates:
      ■ The date coverage would otherwise terminate under the health maintenance contract
      ■ Thirty-six months after the spouse or dependent elected continuation
      ■ The date the spouse or dependent children become covered under another group health plan or Medicare

   b. At no time shall the premium charged exceed 102% of the plan cost. The enrollee is responsible for paying any required fees for coverage on a monthly basis to the group contract holder who will remit payment to the health maintenance organization.

9. **Prohibited practices**

   a. Enrollees must be given 30 days notice of any cancellation or nonrenewal. Enrollees eligible for replacement coverage will receive 90 days notice.

   b. A health maintenance organization may not use any of the following words in its name, contracts, or literature: insurance, casualty, surety, or mutual.

   c. The rates charged by health maintenance organizations and their representatives shall not discriminate except in accordance with accepted actuarial principles. The enrollment policy may not discriminate against recipients of medical assistance or Medicare.

   d. An HMO offering individual or group health maintenance contracts may not refuse to provide or nonrenew coverage because the applicant or enrollee has an option to elect workers' compensation or other disability coverage.

   e. Each health maintenance organization shall establish a telephone number, which need not be toll free, that providers may call with questions about coverage, prior authorization, and approval of medical services. The health maintenance organization must respond to questions within 24 hours after they are received, excluding weekends and holidays.

f. All commissions and other compensation received from the sale or enrollment must be disclosed in writing to the prospective purchaser.

g. An HMO may only cancel or fail to renew coverage of an enrollee for the following reasons:

- Failure to pay the charge for health care coverage
- Termination of the health care plan
- Termination of the group plan
- Enrollee moving out of the service area
- Enrollee moving out of an eligible group
- Failure to make co-payments required by the health care plan
- Fraud or misrepresentation by the enrollee with respect to eligibility for coverage or any other material fact
- Other reasons established in rules promulgated by the Commissioner of health

10. Required replacement coverage When the health maintenance organization terminates the enrollee's individual health coverage, it must offer or arrange to offer replacement coverage, without evidence of insurability, without preexisting condition exclusions, and without interruption of coverage. This requirement applies when the coverage is terminated for a reason other than failure to pay the charge for health care coverage; failure to make the required co-payments; enrollee moving out of the area served; or the enrollee's materially false statement or misrepresentation in the application.

a. The health maintenance organization must provide the terminated enrollee with a notice of cancellation 90 days before the cancellation takes effect. If the replacement coverage is approved by the Commissioner, the notice shall clearly and completely describe the replacement coverage enrollees are eligible to receive and explain the procedure for enrolling. If the replacement coverage is not approved by the Commissioner, the health maintenance organization shall provide a cancellation notice with information that the enrollee is entitled to enroll in the state comprehensive health insurance plan with a waiver of the waiting period for preexisting conditions.

F. NONPROFIT HEALTH SERVICE PLAN CORPORATIONS [62C] A nonprofit service plan corporation can be organized to establish, maintain, and operate a service plan providing health services in their entirety or in part according to the subscriber contract. A service plan corporation may provide for health services by nonparticipating providers in cases of emergency or expediency, or when selected in accordance with the subscriber's contract. When health service is provided out of state, the provider must be licensed, registered, and authorized to provide the service. The rules are quite similar to for-profit health maintenance organizations.

1. A service plan corporation must deliver to every subscriber, except those covered as a spouse or dependent of another subscriber, a copy of the subscriber's contract or a certificate showing that the subscriber is covered by a group subscriber's contract.

2. The subscriber's contract shall clearly state all health services to be provided to the subscriber and all terms, conditions, limitations, and exceptions under which the services shall be provided or for which were paid. The document must also state any provisions for coordination of benefits or subrogation, and any provisions or conditions under which services from participating providers are not covered.

3. Free choice The subscriber is free to choose a provider within a particular class of providers (whether participating or not), and there cannot be any interference with the provider/subscriber relationship.

4. Except for group contracts or certificates, a subscriber's contract shall state the periodic subscription charge, the effective date, the expiration date or period of renewal, and the terms upon which the contract may be terminated, cancelled, continued or renewed.

5. Disabled dependents Coverage through an individual or group contract for dependent children may not be terminated while the child is and continues to be both 1) incapable of self-sustaining employment by reason of developmental disability, mental illness or disorder, or physical disability; and 2) chiefly dependent upon the subscriber or employee for support and maintenance. Proof of the incapacity and dependency must be furnished by the subscriber within 31 days of the child reaching the policy's limiting age and annually thereafter.

6. Maternity benefits Each group or individual contract shall provide the same coverage for maternity benefits to unmarried women and minor female dependents that it provides to married women. If an unmarried subscriber is a parent of a dependent child, each contract shall provide the same coverage for that child as is provided for the child of a married subscriber.

7. Newborn benefits All individual and group contracts must cover a newborn infant immediately from the moment of birth for illness, injury, congenital malformation, or premature birth. Newborn infants include grandchildren who are financially dependent upon a covered grandparent and who reside with the grandparent continuously from birth. Notification to a health carrier is not required to receive this coverage. However, the health carrier is entitled to all additional premiums due. The coverage for newborns includes orthodontic and oral surgery treatment to correct a cleft lip or cleft palate.

8. Divorce A contract providing coverage for the subscriber's spouse may not terminate the spouse's coverage solely as a result of divorce.

    a. Continuation Every subscriber contract shall contain a provision that permits continuation of coverage (for maximum premium not to exceed 102%) for the subscriber's former spouse and children upon furnishing a divorce decree. The coverage shall be continued until the earlier of the following dates:

- The date the subscriber's former spouse becomes covered under any other group health plan
- The date coverage would otherwise terminate under the subscriber contract

b. Conversion Every subscriber contract shall contain a provision allowing the subscriber's former spouse and dependent children, without providing evidence of insurability, to obtain conversion coverage from the health plan. The application and premium payment must be made to the corporation within 30 days following notice of the expiration of the continued coverage.

1.) After January 1, 2014, an individual subscriber contract issued as conversion coverage is renewable at the option of the former spouse as long as the former spouse is not covered under another qualified plan. Any premium rate revisions will be at the former spouse's original age at entry and shall apply equally to all similar contracts issued as conversion coverage.

9. Penalties Any service plan corporation that violates any applicable law is subject to a civil penalty of not more than $5,000 per violation. The Commissioner may also revoke or suspend the insurer's certificate of authority. Any person who makes a material false statement on a written report or statement shall be punished for the first offense by a fine of not more than $1,000 or imprisonment for a maximum of 90 days or both. For the second and each subsequent offense, the fine is not more than $3,000 or imprisonment for not more than one year or both.

G. SMALL EMPLOYER INSURANCE REFORM [62L] Many sections of the state code are impacted by the Affordable Care Act. Some sections are replaced starting January 1, 2014; other sections and subsections are repealed. Effective 2014, every health carrier shall, as a condition of authority to transact business in this state in the small employer market, affirmatively market, offer, sell, issue, and renew any of its health benefit plans, on a guaranteed issue basis, to any small employer.

1. "Employee" means an individual employed for at least 20 hours per week and includes a sole proprietor or a partner of a partnership, if the sole proprietor or partner is included under a health benefit plan of the employer, but does not include individuals who work on a temporary, seasonal, or substitute basis. "Employee" also includes a retiree or a disabled former employee required to be covered.

2. Minnesota will define a "small employer" as, with respect to a calendar year and a plan year, a person, firm, corporation, partnership, association, or other entity actively engaged in business in Minnesota, including a political subdivision of the state, that employed an average of at least one, not including a sole proprietor, but not more than 50 current employees on business days during the preceding calendar year and that employs at least one current employee, not including a sole proprietor, on the first day of the plan year. A small employer plan may be offered through a domiciled association to self-employed individuals and small employers who are members of the association, even if the self-employed individual or small employer has fewer than two current employees. Small employer status must be determined on an annual basis as of the renewal date of the health benefit plan.

a. The provisions of this chapter continue to apply to an employer who no longer meets the requirements of this definition until the annual renewal date of the employer's health benefit plan. If an employer was not in existence throughout the preceding calendar year, the determination of whether the employer is a small employer is based upon the average number of current employees that it is reasonably expected that the employer will employ on business days in the current calendar year. For purposes of this definition, the term *employer* includes any predecessor of the employer.

b. Entities that are treated as a single employer are considered as such for purposes of determining the number of current employees. An employer that has more than 50 current employees but has 50 or fewer employees, as "employee" is defined under federal code, as a small employer under this subdivision. However, small group health plans offered through the Minnesota Insurance Marketplace under chapter 62V are not considered individual health plans, regardless of whether the health plan is purchased using a defined contribution from the small employer. Also, health providers are not obligated to offer plans if employees reside or work outside the providers area(s) of service.

3. Health carriers within the small employer market must issue and renew its health plans on a guaranteed issue basis. This means that a health carrier cannot decline a small employer application for any health benefit plan offered by that health carrier and cannot decline to cover any eligible employee or eligible dependent, including persons who become eligible employees or eligible dependents after initial issuance of the health benefit plan.

4. A small employer that has its workforce reduced to one employee may continue coverage as a small employer for 12 months from the date the group is reduced to one employee.

5. Underwriting restrictions Formerly, these included any refusal of the health carrier to issue or renew coverage, any premium rate higher than the lowest rate charged by the health carrier for the same coverage, any preexisting condition limitation, preexisting condition exclusion, or any exclusionary rider.

a. Health carriers may apply underwriting restrictions to coverage for small employer health benefit plans, including any preexisting condition limitations as permitted by law.

b. Health carriers may collect information relating to the case characteristics and demographic composition of small employers, as well as health status and health history information about small employer employees and dependents.

c. Preexisting conditions may be excluded by a health carrier up to 12 months from the enrollment date of an eligible employee or dependent. Exclusionary riders may not be used.

d. Late entrants may be subject to a preexisting condition limitation not to exceed 18 months from the enrollment date of the late entrant, but may not be subject to any exclusionary rider or preexisting condition exclusion. Beginning January 1, 2014, plans may no longer segregate "late entrants."

e. Health carriers may not use pregnancy as a preexisting condition.

f. Under the Affordable Care Act, according to HF 779, (January 1, 2014) it states that, "all plans will be guaranteed issued," so any references to preexisting conditions will be repealed.

6. **Minimum participation and contribution** A small employer that has at least 75% of its eligible employees who have not waived coverage participating in a health benefit plan and that contributes at least 50% toward the cost of coverage of each eligible employee must be guaranteed coverage on a guaranteed issue basis from any health carrier participating in the small employer market. The participation level of eligible employees must be determined at the initial offering of coverage and at the renewal date of coverage.

   a. A health carrier must not increase the participation requirements at any time after the group has been accepted for coverage.

   b. A "waiver of coverage" includes only waivers due to:
   - coverage under another group health plan;
   - coverage under Medicare Parts A and B; or
   - coverage under medical assistance or general assistance medical care.

   c. If a small employer does not satisfy the contribution or participation requirements, it may voluntarily issue or renew individual health plans or a health benefit plan that must fully comply with 62L. However, small employers not meeting participation requirements may purchase coverage only during an open enrollment period each year between November 15 and December 15.

7. **Cancellations and failures to renew** A health carrier cannot cancel, decline to issue, or fail to renew a health benefit plan because of the claim experience or health status of the persons covered, or to be covered, by the health benefit plan.

   a. However, a health carrier may cancel or nonrenew a health benefit plan:
   - for nonpayment of premium;
   - for fraud or misrepresentation by the small employer with respect to eligibility for coverage or any other material fact; or
   - if the employer fails to comply with the minimum contribution percentage required.

   b. Following January 1, 2014, insurers may nonrenew:
   - if eligible employee participation during the preceding calendar year declines to less than 75%;
   - if the health carrier ceases to do business in the small employer market; or

■   if a failure to renew is based on the insurer's decision to discontinue the health benefit plan form. However, nonrenewal may only occur if the carrier permits each employer covered under the prior form to switch to its choice of any other health benefit plan offered by the health carrier, without any underwriting restrictions.

8. **Continuation and dependent coverage** Small employer plans must include the continuation of coverage provisions required by COBRA. Other state law and rules applicable to health plan coverage of newborn infants, dependent children who do not reside with the eligible employee, disabled children and dependents, and adopted children apply to a small employer plan.

9. **Disclosure of underwriting practices** When offering or renewing a health benefit plan, health carriers shall disclose the following in all solicitation and sales materials:

   ■   Provisions concerning the health carrier's right to change premium rates

   ■   Provisions relating to renewability of coverage

   ■   The application of any provider network limitations and their effect on eligibility for benefits

   ■   The ability of small employers to insure eligible employees and dependents currently receiving coverage from the Comprehensive Health Association

10. **Small employer requirements** Health benefit plans must require that small employers offering a health benefit plan maintain information verifying the continuing eligibility of the employer, its employees, and their dependents, and provide the information to health carriers on a quarterly basis or as reasonably requested by the health carrier. In addition, small employers offering a health benefit plan must maintain written documentation indicating that each eligible employee was informed of the availability of coverage through the employer and documentation that the eligible employee waived coverage.

11. **Prohibited practices** A health carrier operating in the small employer market should not knowingly offer, issue, or renew an individual health plan to an eligible employee of a small employer that meets the minimum participation and contribution requirements. Exceptions include the following.

   ■   The employee leaves an HMO's service area.

   ■   The plan is offered to the employee as a continuation or conversion of expiring coverage.

   ■   A health carrier may sell, issue, or renew an individual health plan if coverage provided by the employer is determined to be unaffordable under the provisions of the Affordable Care Act.

   ■   The individual health plan is a high deductible health plan for use in connection with an existing health savings account (HSA). In that situation, the same or a different health carrier may offer, issue, sell, or renew a group health plan to cover the other eligible employees in the group.

■ The individual health plan is marketed directly to all employees of the small employer, and the small employer does not contribute directly or indirectly to the premiums or facilitate the administration of the individual health plan.

12. Penalties The Commissioner may suspend or revoke a health carrier's license or certificate of authority and impose a monetary penalty not to exceed $25,000 for each violation of the statute.

13. Policy discontinuation A health carrier electing to cease doing business in the small employer market must notify the Commissioner and each small employer covered 180 days in advance. The insurance carrier must renew its current small employer business that is due for renewal within 120 days after notifying the Commissioner. In addition, the health carrier cannot write new business in the Minnesota small employer market for five years from the date of notification to the Commissioner. *Ceasing to do business* means not issuing new benefit plans and not renewing existing benefit plans.

MINNESOTA LAW SUPPLEMENT PRACTICE FINAL

Student instructions: Following your thorough study of this supplement, take this 50-question sample examination. Grade your performance utilizing the answer key provided. Carefully review the topics pertaining to those questions answered incorrectly.

I. General Insurance

1. Which statement accurately describes the required conduct of an agent?
   A. An agent is required to deliver an insured's policy within 10 business days.
   B. Producer's are allowed to disclose their customers' names provided they do not identify the policy they have purchased.
   C. A producer may accept a loan from a customer provided the agreement is in writing and all records are kept for at least 6 years after repayment.
   D. Oral binders must be followed up in writing within 7 business days.

2. In the case of a deceased licensed insurance producer, the Commissioner may extend a temporary insurance producer license to the administrator or executor for a period not to exceed a total of how many days?
   A. 60
   B. 90
   C. 180
   D. 365

3. A licensed insurance producer, limited lines producer, or temporary insurance producer who is convicted of a felony must report it to the Commissioner within how many days of the conviction?
   A. 10
   B. 21
   C. 30
   D. 45

4. Which of the following is NOT included in the broad powers of the Commissioner of Commerce?
   A. Making rules and regulations as necessary to implement the insurance laws
   B. Conducting examinations as needed to determine whether a person or company has violated any insurance law or regulation
   C. Instituting such actions or other lawful proceedings as deemed necessary to enforce the state's insurance laws and regulations
   D. Developing and writing insurance education courses

5. What is the daily fine that may be assessed against a person who disobeys a cease and desist order of the Commissioner?
   A. $1,000
   B. $5,000
   C. $10,000
   D. $20,000

6. The Commissioner will examine the affairs and conditions of every insurer licensed in Minnesota at least once every how many years?
   A. 1
   B. 3
   C. 5
   D. 7

7. When can a licensed producer sell an insurance policy without a company appointment?
   A. If the producer has the insurer's permission and obtains an appointment within 15 days of submitting the first application
   B. When the producer has the insurer's written permission
   C. When the producer has permission from the Commissioner
   D. The producer is not allowed to transact any insurance business without a company appointment.

8. How many years must an insurance company maintain documentation of an advertisement used in promoting a life insurance policy or annuity?

    A. 3
    B. 4
    C. 5
    D. 7

9. If the Commissioner refuses to renew a producer's license, a written notice is issued. Which of the following statements about the notice is NOT correct?

    A. The notice will state the grounds for which the license was not renewed.
    B. The notice will state the possible criminal charges that may result from the licensee's actions.
    C. The notice will advise the producer to request a hearing within 30 days.
    D. The hearing will be held within 30 days of the producer's written request.

10. Which of the following statements about mutual insurers is NOT correct?

    A. Mutual insurance companies are managed by a board of directors
    B. Mutual insurance companies return taxable dividends to policyholders
    C. Mutual insurance companies are legal reserve companies
    D. Mutual insurance companies are owned by their policyholders

11. An agent whose license is revoked will be ineligible to reapply for any license for how many years?

    A. 1
    B. 2
    C. 3
    D. 5

12. As established by law, the fee for an accident and health producer license is

    A. $50 every year
    B. $100 every year
    C. $50 every 2 years
    D. $100 every 2 years

13. Applicants for insurance producer licensing must meet all of the following requirements EXCEPT

    A. be age 18
    B. be competent, trustworthy, and of good business reputation
    C. complete an approved prelicensing course of study
    D. comply with the bond requirement

14. Which of the following statements about continuing education requirements in Minnesota is NOT correct?

    A. The producer must complete at least 3 credit hours in the area of ethics.
    B. Only continuing education courses offered in a classroom setting are approved for credit.
    C. All continuing education courses must be approved by the Commissioner before they can be offered to producers for credit.
    D. After being licensed, insurance producers must satisfactorily complete 24 hours of approved continuing education during each licensing period.

15. The Minnesota Guaranty Fund was established to protect all of the following EXCEPT

    A. policyowners
    B. insurance companies
    C. annuitants
    D. beneficiaries

16. All the following individuals are required to become licensed in order to practice in the insurance business in Minnesota EXCEPT

    A. nonresident producers who hold the CLU® designation
    B. a salaried employee who advises an employer about insurance matters and does not receive a commission
    C. a business entity acting as an insurance producer
    D. limited lines producers

17. Under Minnesota law, all of the following are defined as unfair claims practices by insurance companies EXCEPT
    A. failing to promptly acknowledge pertinent communications concerning claims
    B. delaying an investigation or claim payment by requiring a duplicate verification of facts
    C. compelling policyowners to go to court to recover amounts due them by offering them substantially less than the amounts recovered through litigation
    D. offering payment of approved claims after affirming liability

18. Regarding company claims practices, which of the following statements is NOT correct?
    A. When denying a claim, the insurer is required to reference the applicable policy language in the denial letter.
    B. A company may require an inspection at a location convenient to the insured.
    C. An insurer who responds within 7 days to an insured's voicemail has not violated a claim settlement practice.
    D. To make a correct negligence assignment, the insurer can require ancillary information in addition to the loss information.

19. In Minnesota, to be an admitted company means the insurer has which of the following?
    A. Certificate of authority
    B. Company appointment
    C. Surplus license
    D. Reciprocal license

20. An agent must retain complaint and financial records for how many years?
    A. 2
    B. 4
    C. 6
    D. Indefinitely

21. An example of unfair discrimination is best demonstrated by which of the following situations?
    A. An insurer refuses to reinstate a National Guard member's life insurance policy after coverage was nonrenewed while the person was on active duty.
    B. An insurer refuses to issue a policy to an applicant who has had 5 liability claims in the previous 3 years.
    C. An insurer assigns a premium rating to an applicant who weighs 30 pounds more than a typical person of that age and gender.
    D. An insurer refuses to issue a policy to an applicant whose credit history suggests an inability to financially support the policy for which the applicant is applying.

22. Which of the following statements about nonresident agents is CORRECT?
    A. A nonresident agent must take the Minnesota licensing examination to transact insurance in Minnesota.
    B. An individual who holds a producer license in a home state, and whose state issues nonresident licenses to Minnesota residents on the same basis may apply for a nonresident license in Minnesota.
    C. A nonresident agent must file an affidavit with the Commerce Department that appoints the Commissioner of a home state as an agent for service of process in any legal proceeding.
    D. A nonresident agent must take the same pre-licensing education that resident agents complete.

23. A temporary license can be issued to all of the following EXCEPT
    A. an employee of a business entity upon the disability of the individual designated on the license
    B. an individual who has passed the producer exam and is waiting for a license to be issued
    C. the producer's spouse in order to renew insurance business sold by the deceased
    D. a businesses partner chosen by the Commissioner to perform tasks incidental to insurance business in force at the time of death

24. How long does an insurance producer's license remain valid in Minnesota?

    A. For as long as the 2-year licensing period, after which it must be renewed with another round of license testing
    B. As long as the appointing insurance company pays the appropriate fee each January 1
    C. Continually, as long as the renewal fees are paid, and the continuing education requirements are met
    D. Until revoked by the appointing insurer

25. A producer must inform the Commissioner of any change to the producer's residential address within how many days of the change?

    A. 10
    B. 20
    C. 30
    D. 60

II. Life Insurance

26. When an agent sells a life insurance policy, the agent is allowed to backdate the policy up to how many months?

    A. 1
    B. 3
    C. 6
    D. 12

27. The policyowner may cancel a whole life policy within how many days of receiving it?

    A. 5
    B. 10
    C. 20
    D. 30

28. Which of the following statements about group life insurance is NOT correct?

    A. An employee's group term life policy will terminate if the employee is laid off.
    B. COBRA-like rules apply to group term life insurance.
    C. Group life insurance paid by the employer typically does not require proof of insurability.
    D. Terminated employees may elect to continue group term life coverage for themselves and their dependents.

29. If an employer fails to notify a terminated employee of the option to continue group term life coverage

    A. the employee loses the opportunity to continue coverage
    B. the employer must provide the employee with a permanent life insurance policy
    C. the employee has an additional 60 days to elect to continue coverage
    D. the employer is liable for the employee's coverage just as the insurer would be if coverage were still in effect

30. Which provision allows an individual life insurance policy to stay in force in the event the premium payment is late?

    A. Ownership provision
    B. Grace period provision
    C. Free-look provision
    D. Premium waiver provision

31. Under the grace period provision, how will the overdue premium be handled if the insured dies during the grace period?

    A. Any premium due will be waived
    B. The policyowner will owe twice the amount due
    C. If any premium is owed at the time of the insured's death, the policy will be cancelled
    D. The overdue premium will be deducted from the settlement

32. All of the following are true statements regarding the insurance company's right to cancel a life insurance policy EXCEPT

    A. the policy must include a notice regarding the policyowner's rights to cancel the policy
    B. after receiving notice of cancellation from the insured, the insurer must refund all premiums paid within 10 days
    C. if the policyowner cancels a replacement life insurance policy 20 days after receiving it, the insurer is not required to refund any premium
    D. if a policy is sold without a notice regarding cancellation, it may be cancelled by the purchaser at any time within one year after the purchase date

33. The free-look provision on a joint life policy begins
    A. when the first person dies
    B. when the policy is delivered to the policyowner
    C. on the issue date of the policy
    D. on the date of the application

III. Accident and Health Insurance

34. An agent-solicited Medicare supplement policy must contain a printed notice that the insured, if not satisfied for any reason, has how many days after delivery in which to return the policy for a refund?
    A. 7
    B. 10
    C. 14
    D. 30

35. Which of the following statements concerning individual accident and health insurance policies is CORRECT?
    A. Insurer's must cover adopted children on the same basis as other dependents.
    B. Upon a divorce, the insured's former spouse is no longer covered by the insured's individual health insurance policy.
    C. The insured must wait 90 days after proof of loss to sue the insurer.
    D. Individual health policies can be more restrictive when covering chemical dependency services.

36. An accident or health insurance policy may not be rescinded, except for fraud, after it has been in effect for
    A. 6 months
    B. 1 year
    C. 2 years
    D. 4 years

37. When selling a health benefit plan to a small employer, insurers must make, as part of their solicitation and sales material, a reasonable disclosure of all the following EXCEPT
    A. provisions relating to policy renewability
    B. information relating to the insurer's reserve requirements
    C. provisions relating to preexisting conditions
    D. provisions concerning the insurer's right to change premiums

38. A Medicare supplement insurance policy application was taken on March 16. The insurer issued the policy on March 28, and it was delivered to the policyowner on April 5. Under these circumstances, when does the policy's free-look period end?
    A. March 26
    B. April 15
    C. April 27
    D. May 5

39. Qualified long-term care insurance policies sold in Minnesota must include a renewability provision that is at least as favorable as a provision that makes the policy
    A. cancellable
    B. renewable at the insurer's option
    C. guaranteed renewable (premiums may be increased)
    D. noncancellable (premiums cannot be increased)

40. A Medicare supplement policy is issued on May 1. Until what date must the insurer cover preexisting conditions, if it chooses to use the maximum time allowed under Minnesota law?
    A. June 1
    B. August 1
    C. November 1
    D. May 1 of the following year

41. All of the following are required provisions of an accident and health policy EXCEPT
    A. physical exam and autopsy provision
    B. change of beneficiary provision
    C. grace period provision
    D. misstatement of age provision

42. Individual health policies offered through the Minnesota Comprehensive Health Association (MCHA) provide coverage for Minnesota residents denied coverage by the private market. Which of the following statements about MCHA is NOT correct?

    A. Pre-existing conditions for individuals insured through the plan can be excluded during the first 6 months of coverage
    B. MCHA provides coverage if benefits are payable under Medicare
    C. Premiums charged to policyholders are higher than rates on comparable policies in the private market
    D. MCHA policies offer high deductible health plans and basic Medicare supplement policies

43. The penalties for violating the laws governing the sale of Medicare supplements in Minnesota can include

    A. imprisonment for up to 3 years
    B. fines up to $1,000
    C. fines up to $2,500
    D. fines up to $5,000

44. When a Medicare supplement policyholder applies for and is entitled to Medicaid benefits, Medicare supplement policies

    A. provide enhanced benefits
    B. must provide for a suspension of benefits and premiums for up to 24 months
    C. are automatically cancelled
    D. increase dramatically in premium cost

45. All of the following must be provided to a long-term care policy applicant at or before application EXCEPT

    A. suitability standards
    B. outline of coverage
    C. long-term care insurance Shopper's Guide
    D. long-term care insurance Personal Worksheet

46. All of the following illnesses, treatments, or conditions can be limited or excluded from coverage on a qualified long-term care policy EXCEPT

    A. treatment for chemical dependency
    B. benefits covered by another long-term care policy covering the insured
    C. expenses that are reimbursable through Social Security
    D. benefits provided for Alzheimer's disease

47. If an enrollee and spouse divorce, a health maintenance contract that provides coverage for the enrollee's spouse will

    A. terminate coverage for the former spouse but not for the dependents
    B. terminate upon the divorce
    C. incur a premium increase up to 150% of the plan cost if the former spouse continues coverage
    D. allow the former spouse to continue coverage

48. A long-term care policy

    A. may not exclude coverage for adult day care services
    B. must provide a free-look period of 20 days
    C. can be cancelled by the insurer if the insured's health deteriorates
    D. covers all nursing home and home care costs

49. Up until full implementation of the Affordable Care Act, health carriers selling plans to small employers are allowed to

    A. use pregnancy as a pre-existing condition
    B. exclude an eligible employee's pre-existing condition up to 12 months from the enrollment date
    C. include exclusionary riders in the policy
    D. place a pre-existing condition limitation of 24 months on an individual who is a late entrant to the enrollment period

50. All of the following are correct about coverage through a health maintenance organization EXCEPT

    A. the annual open enrollment period lasts a minimum of 14 days, during which eligible individuals have the opportunity to enroll for coverage
    B. services provided by any medical provider are covered by the health maintenance organization
    C. individual policies contain a 31-day grace period during which the policy will remain in force if the premium is late
    D. enrollees may be expected to pay co-payments

ANSWERS TO MINNESOTA LAW PRACTICE FINAL

1. C	11. B	21. A	31. D	41. D
2. C	12. C	22. B	32. C	42. B
3. A	13. D	23. B	33. B	43. D
4. D	14. B	24. C	34. D	44. B
5. C	15. B	25. A	35. A	45. A
6. C	16. B	26. C	36. C	46. D
7. A	17. D	27. B	37. B	47. D
8. A	18. D	28. A	38. D	48. A
9. B	19. A	29. D	39. C	49. B
10. B	20. C	30. B	40. C	50. B